AT
HOME
IN THE
WORLD

D0062888

AT

HOME

IN THE

WORLD

THE LETTERS OF

THOMAS MERTON & ROSEMARY RADFORD RUETHER

Edited by
MARY TARDIFF, O.P.

ORBIS BOOKS

Maryknoll, New York 10545

The Catholic Foreign Mission Society of America (Maryknoll) recruits and trains people for overseas missionary service. Through Orbis Books, Maryknoll aims to foster the international dialogue that is essential to mission. The books published, however, reflect the opinions of their authors and are not meant to represent the official position of the society.

Copyright © 1995 by Rosemary Radford Ruether and Mary Tardiff, O.P.

The publisher wishes gratefully to acknowledge the cooperation of the Thomas Merton Legacy Trust, Farrar, Straus & Giroux, and HarperCollins Publishers Limited (London) for permission to reprint the letters of Thomas Merton.

Published by Orbis Books, Maryknoll, NY 10545-0308

All rights reserved. No part of this publication may be reproduced or transmitted in any form or by any means, electronic or mechanical, including photocopying, recording, or any information storage or retrieval system, without prior permission in writing from the publishers.

Queries regarding rights and permissions should be addressed to: Orbis Books, P.O. Box 308, Maryknoll, NY 10545-0308. Queries regarding the letters of Thomas Merton should be addressed to Farrar Straus & Giroux, 19 Union Sq. W, New York, NY 10003.

Manufactured in the United States of America

Cataloging-in-Publication Data is available from the Library of Congress, Washington, D.C.

ISBN 1-57075-015-7

CONTENTS

PREFACE

*T*he existence of this correspondence between Rosemary Radford Ruether and Thomas Merton first came to my attention while doing research for my doctoral dissertation on the theological method of Rosemary Ruether. Its discovery excited me for several reasons. One rather obvious one was the direct relationship between the correspondence and my own research. Because my own research has been on Rosemary Ruether, my comments in this Preface will focus on her. Ruether herself has written an excellent Introduction contextualizing the correspondence through her own memory of it. The Afterword by Christine Bochen shifts the focus to Merton and helps to explain what was happening in his life during these years of letter writing. Autobiographical information on either Ruether or Merton is available elsewhere.[1]

While Merton's letters to Ruether were published in 1985 in *The Hidden Ground of Love,* edited by William H. Shannon, and excerpts of Ruether's letters to Merton appeared in Monica Furlong's *Merton: A Biography,* Ruether's side of the correspondence, let alone a complete documentation, has never been published. This may be the only collection of Ruether letters that we will ever have. There is no similar correspondence still extant today,

---

1. Rosemary Ruether, *Disputed Questions: On Being a Christian* (Maryknoll, N.Y.: Orbis Books, 1989); Thomas Merton, *Conjectures of a Guilty Bystander* (New York: Doubleday, 1968), as well as his published letters and several biographical works.

and, as Ruether says in her Introduction, "the tradition of extensive letter writing is not much practiced these days, at least by myself." These letters make a positive contribution to a specific literary genre and constitute a unique contribution to the historical, theological, and ecclesiological understanding of the late 1960s.

At that time, the Roman Catholic Church had just made numerous pronouncements resulting from its Second Vatican Council, a council of renewal and the first council to be held in almost one hundred years. In its wake hopes were high for changes in all aspects of ecclesial life, especially the liturgy, the role of women, the church's role in the growing ecumenical movement, and its relationship to a modern world that it had all but ignored. In the United States Catholic theologians had been influenced by several current intellectual trends, such as the rise of secular theology and the thought of those who would proclaim that, to modern humanity, "God is dead." Such a turn to the reality of the secular nature of our society also issued in a theological concern for the issues affecting our society: crises in the civil rights movement, conscientious objectors and the nature of the war in Vietnam, countercultural movements ushering in the sexual revolution, and a general upheaval of established values.

When her correspondence with Thomas Merton began, Rosemary Ruether was in the thick and at the theological forefront of these events, though it was highly unusual for a Roman Catholic woman, let alone a laywoman with three children, to acquire theological credentials. She had just finished her doctoral degree in classics and patristics through the Claremont Graduate School in Claremont, California. She, together with her three children and her husband, Herman, were leaving California and moving to Washington, D.C. By the following fall she had embarked upon what would be a ten-year academic post as professor of historical theology at Howard University. She and her family lived and worshiped in a mixed, largely black neighborhood.

One will notice through these letters that from the beginning of her professional career Ruether never hesitated to speak radical words or engage in radical actions.To this day she uses her theological skills on behalf of those who do not have a voice. Since 1976 she has been the Georgia Harkness Professor of Applied Theology at Garrett-Evangelical Theological Seminary in Evanston, Illinois. She is internationally known as a speaker and writer who addresses the significant issues of the day. She is especially recognized as a feminist theologian, though the reader will note that her letters to Merton indicate a period prior to her more developed feminist consciousness.

Though this exchange of letters is rich enough to stand on its own, I would like to emphasize three interrelated areas that promise a more comprehensive understanding of Rosemary Ruether, namely, biography, theology, and method. The claim has been made, and rightfully so, that one's personal life is integrally related to one's theological interests and method. In other words, biography is formative of theology. Though these letters were never intended to be autobiographical in a formal sense, the very nature of informal letter writing lends itself to self-revelation on a personal level. Though engaged in a discussion of theological issues, Ruether is constantly drawing on personal experiences, disclosing profound intuitions and deeply held personal convictions. For example, the intensity of her questions regarding identification with the poor emerge from her experiences of urban ghetto life and reveal her convictions about "a fatal contradiction between simultaneously idealizing poverty and working to overcome other people's poverty." A close attention to Ruether's existential situation will disclose for the reader the experiential underpinnings of her theological questions.

Ruether's theological interests were, and are, as varied as her personal involvements. This is perceived most clearly when one considers the general content of the correspondence. Though Ruether and Merton candidly discuss several significant theological issues, it is obvious that Merton's overriding concern is monastic renewal. Other issues, such as ecclesial renewal, radicalism, sexuality, racism, ecumenism, and poverty, are woven into the conversation by Ruether. Her initial ruminations regarding Scripture, christology, ecclesiology, eschatology, and social morality are often interjected in the process of "working out an idea in a letter." Though many of these ideas come to greater fruition in her later articles and books, she does not hesitate to engage such great theological figures as Augustine, Luther, Loisy, Bonhoeffer, and Teilhard de Chardin in the conversation at hand. References to them are as common as references to Daniel Berrigan, Gabriel Vahanian, Thomas Altizer, and Charles Davis, all contemporaries of Ruether and Merton.

The insightful reader will also discover that Ruether's experiences of certain contradictions (such as the one mentioned above in relation to poverty) not only give rise to her theology but also give form to a rudimentary theological method. Ruether casts these contradictions in the mold of false dualisms, such as clergy-laity, city-country, church-world, creation-world, historical-charismatic. These dualisms are false because, instead of representing the true dynamic and creative potential that the elements have for dealing with reality, they are portrayed as static poles of our existence and thus reveal a destructive bias for one side as better than the other. The reader will discover Ruether ferreting out the truth content of each dualism's neglected side, putting the poles into a dialectical relationship, and forming dynamic unities that serve as the impetus for positive actions on behalf of church and society.

Because Ruether believed such dualisms to be perpetuated by abstract thought, she considered any "ivory tower" theology as subject to suspicion. She clearly asserts, "I distrust all academic theology. Only theology bred in the crucible of experience is any good." For Ruether, our understanding regarding the role of experience is directly related to the value we place on ourselves as historical beings. If we believe that God's self-revelation occurs in history, in our personal and communal experiences, then "the main arena of salvation," the locus of God's redemptive activity, takes place "in the sphere of historical action."

Besides drawing attention to the intellectual content of these letters, I have attempted to capture their overall spirit. I have tried to achieve a holistic context through the inclusion of three circular letters (two from Merton and one from Ruether), explanatory footnotes, and brief pieces of information that are bracketed within the text; a copy of one of the Merton drawings that is discussed in the later letters has also been included. A chronological and dialogical presentation will enable an orderly reading of the correspondence. Since Ruether did not date her letters, the dates assigned to them in this collection have been drawn from internal evidence or the postal cancellation on the envelope.

After Merton typed his letters, he frequently reread them and made editorial changes on the originals that were not made on the carbons. At the time that Shannon edited Merton's correspondence, copies of the original letters were not available. In preparing this manuscript I was able to procure copies of Merton's original letters. Hence, though not of major consequence, this volume does incorporate the hand-written additions, deletions, and marginal jottings for which Merton is well known. It also includes a hand-written letter that did not appear in *The Hidden Ground of Love*. It is one that Merton wrote while still in the hospital (March 4, 1967). Besides the two circular letters mentioned above, his "My Campaign Platform" and a poem, "A Round and a Hope for Smithgirls," are also included.

I wish to express my gratitude to Robert E. Daggy, director of the Thomas Merton Studies Center, for his prompt and generous assistance in procuring copies of Ruether's original letters to Merton. Thanks are also due to William H. Shannon, who has not only supplied some references and corrections to the original typescript, but has given valuable advice and been a supporter of this project from its inception. Without the contribution made by Christine Bochen we would be lacking some very insightful comments that give a broader scope to Merton's life and thought. For this, I thank her. I am most grateful to Rosemary Ruether. She has generously shared copies of her original Merton letters, supplied clarifications, corrected errors in the original typescript, arranged for the art, and contributed a most informative contextualization of these letters in her Introduction to the book. A special word of appreciation is always due one's editor. Robert Ellsberg has been indomitable in his enthusiasm, advice, encouragement, and gentle reminders regarding deadlines. It has been a pleasure to work with him on this project. These acknowledgments would not be complete without an expression of gratitude to Nancy Burkin, S.S.J., who provided the ongoing encouragement and support that brought this work to completion.

INTRODUCTION

by Rosemary Radford Ruether

*I*t is always a strange experience to encounter yourself as you were twenty-eight years ago. Since the tradition of extensive letter writing is not much practiced these days, at least by myself, the very fact that Thomas Merton and I even gave the time to such extensive correspondence over an eighteen-month period is itself somewhat awesome. In this brief introduction, I wish to say some things to help the reader put this correspondence in its appropriate context, at least for myself, and perhaps for Merton as well.

However, let me say at the outset that I am not a Merton scholar and perhaps not even a Merton "fan." I have not read everything that he has written, and most of what I have read was quite some years ago, even before the years of this brief correspondence between us. This is not intended to suggest any disrespect for his corpus of writings, but rather simply to indicate that, in a real sense, much of his writings belonged to an earlier, pre–Vatican II generation of Catholicism and a struggle with monastic life of that earlier period. Thus it is probably more appropriate for genuine Merton scholars than for myself to try to put Merton's own letters in the context of his life work.

I had had a brief and superficial interest in monastic life through my relation with the Benedictine priory of St. Andrew's in Valyermo, California, in the early 1960s. At the time when these letters were written I had become disillusioned with what such monastic community could offer me as a laywoman, especially because of the rather brutal treatment of Father Vincent Martin, O.S.B., who had been the director of the oblates at Valyermo (see the letter of mid-February 1967). In 1966 I was immersed in teaching at a black theological seminary at an urban university (Howard University School of Religion) and working in urban churches on issues of racism, poverty, and militarism.

Although I can't speak with authority on the subject of where Merton was "at" at the time of these letters, it appeared to me then, and still does today, that he himself was at the end of a period of development of his own thinking on monasticism, within the context of Gethsemani, and was very much testing the waters to explore what he should do next. What this next stage of his life should be was certainly very unresolved, at least within the framework of this period of correspondence. He had a sense that he needed to get out and go somewhere else, but just where and how it could be legitimated by the order was uncertain.

I think that there is no doubt that the next stage of life he had in mind was still within the framework of monastic life, but some new context of monastic life that would not burden him with unreasonable restrictions, such as he clearly suffered from his abbot, and also where he would be more in touch with lively currents of thought and the crucial social conflicts of the times, such as a setting in Latin America. (A community in Chile is mentioned several times in the letters, but not identified.)

One thing that came across to me in the letters at the time, and again in rereading them, is that he was extremely apprehensive about simply being thrown into the world with its vast array of choices. Monasticism, even with its restrictions, seemed to offer him a kind of protection from what he seemed to fear outside as an exploitative environment that would lionize him as a celebrity, but not give him the space for authentic life. Thus what he seemed to be looking for was, not to leave monastic life, but to discover a new stage of monastic life that would offer him the needed ambiance for new growth, without dropping him into the temptations of an uncontrolled environment.

Exactly what that new stage of monastic life might have been, had Merton lived, I think cannot be decided, at least by these letters. He was obviously very anxious about making an inauthentic choice. He preferred to make no choice and to remain in what was, in many ways, a demeaning environment, rather than make the wrong choice. In one later letter (which apparently has not been preserved) I even jokingly suggested to him that the reason he could not make the choice to leave Gethsemani was that he had so many books and papers there it would take a train to dig him out! But that was just a figurative way of saying that he had a lot of things (and not just in weight of paper) that were keeping him in the situation where he was at that time.

I am on sounder ground in talking about where I was "at" at the time of this correspondence, rather than where Merton was at. I was twenty-nine years old when this correspondence began and barely thirty-one when it ended, due to his untimely death during his Asian journey at the end of 1968. Thus this correspondence took place when I was just at the beginning of my intellectual career as a thinker and writer, while he was at the end of a major stage of his life and writing career and was to be cut off before he could enter what might have been a new stage of development of his later years.

What comes across in these letters is that, although we were separated by more than twenty years in age, he as a seasoned thinker and I as a neophyte, Merton from the beginning addressed me as an equal. (This did not surprise me at the time, since I saw myself as an equal, but it is more impressive in retrospect.) Occasionally he assumed the stance of subordinate, asking me to be his teacher or even confessor. But never did he take the paternalistic stance as the father addressing the child, which is more typical of the cleric, especially in relation to women.

Mostly, in these letters, we dialogue and even scrap with each other as intellectual siblings.

What I was looking for in initiating this conversation was neither a confessor, nor to be his confessor, but a genuine Catholic intellectual peer, one who would treat me as a peer, and with whom I could be ruthlessly honest about my own questions of intellectual and existential integrity. I was trying to test in this correspondence what was the crucial issue, for me, at that time: whether it was, in fact, actually possible to be a Roman Catholic and to be a person of integrity.

If there is a certain shocking style of frankness in these letters, it was because, for me, it was very important to explore this question with at least one committed Roman Catholic intellectual of "advanced" spiritual development. It was in the quest of an answer to that question that I engaged in what might be seen as a kind of ruthless questioning of Merton's own integrity. For me the issue was this: if such a man could not be a person of integrity and a Catholic, could anyone be?

I had explored this question with a number of Roman Catholic leaders during my college years, ranging from my parish priest to Msgr. Fulton Sheen. To my great disgust Fulton Sheen was so incapable of taking seriously my questions and the papers I sent him that I received only a curt letter from his secretary suggesting that I only wanted his autograph! Most of these clerical gentlemen, and an occasional nun, ended the conversation suggesting I should "pray for faith," a response that struck me as a covert invitation to shut down my mind.

In the mid-1960s the Second Vatican Council began to break open the repressed doubts and questions of Catholics and allowed a much freer and more open conversation to take place. Many of the questions that I had been asking as a college student and that seemed beyond the pale of discussion, now were open to debate. I increasingly was able to raise my sights and to engage in conversation with persons who were shaping the new conversation of Catholicism, such as Daniel Berrigan and Gregory Baum.

Others who seemed as coming lights, such as Robert Adolfs in Holland, would drop out of the picture, themselves victims of contradictions they would not be able to hold together.

Yet even with conversations with such persons I felt a deep sense of disappointment, a feeling that the critical questions of integrity were easily glossed over, even by reforming Catholics. Could Catholics, for example, really face the question that was apparent to those who studied critical New Testament exegesis, namely, that Jesus probably didn't intend to found any separate Christian religion at all, much less any institution with the structure of the Roman Catholic Church? In the face of such a radical need to question foundations, the pretenses of papal infallibility appeared like a bad joke.

The question for me was not simply historical truth, but truthful living in the light of such questions and uncertainties. Could Catholics speak the truth and be Catholics? That Christians err, and even create monstrous idolatries, was in itself not scandalous to me. That seemed to be only human. What was scandalous and insupportable was to be unable to admit error, to be incapable of repentance because you cannot entertain the possibility that you might be wrong. Worse still, to make such incapacity for self-questioning a dogma! That for me was the crux of the Catholic dilemma.

In retrospect I might say that, for me, in 1966 Merton was my "test case" for whether integrity was possible for Catholics. I wanted to raise with him all my questions and doubts and see if he could "handle" them. Such probing must have been something of a surprise to him, but it also seemed to have arrived in his life at a time when he also needed to ask himself some searching questions. The questions he needed to ask himself were rather different from the questions I wanted to ask him in reference to my own life, so our conversations many times were more a bouncing off each other than a connecting.

In Monica Furlong's much publicized book *Merton: A Biography,* she surmises that this correspondence was extremely important to Merton and a kind of breakthrough experience of honest repartee with a woman. This may be true, but it is important for me to say that Furlong, for whatever reason, never discussed her thesis with me and so I knew it only after the book was published. In my own mind I did not take this correspondence to be particularly important to Merton. I assumed that he corresponded with hundreds of people all over the world, and I was only one of many.

In Merton's correspondence there are many form letters to his many correspondents, in which he apologized for not being able to write them personal letters. Because he sometimes wrote me very long letters the same day as he made such apologies, it is clear that he was indeed giving more than a small amount of time to this correspondence for a brief period of time. Perhaps it became for him an occasion for trying to sort out some questions about his own integrity of life that he needed to surface for himself.

I experienced at the time, and again in reading this correspondence, that there was a certain intensity that peaked about May 1967. I remember beginning to feel disappointed, feeling that he really didn't want to look more deeply at the "box" he was in. The correspondence after this point becomes more rote. I discuss incidents of my work in the city that he enjoys and we become involved in working on the disposition of some paintings he has done and wants to extract from an art dealer who he fears is exploiting them.

Interestingly enough, our conversation begins to fade in intensity exactly at the moment when Merton suggests that we might become collaborators more publicly, taping a conversation on monasticism that might be published. Perhaps it became apparent to him that what I wanted to discuss and what he wanted to discuss were not really on the same wave length. Part of this was simply that we were at different stages of life. In a later letter he backed away from the suggestion of collaboration, and I was not that anxious to pursue it either.

I never met Thomas Merton. The one time I hoped to meet him did not work out, and he was not to return alive from his trip to Asia in 1968. I have no idea whether, if he had lived, we would have developed some more public collaboration. I don't even know that we would have liked each other that much if we had met. My sense is, however, that we would not have returned to the intensity of the conversation of the letters of the previous year.

I see Thomas Merton and myself somewhat like two ships that happened to pass each other on our respective journeys. For a brief moment we turned our search lights on each other with blazing intensity. Then, when we sensed that we were indeed going in different directions, we began to pass each other by. Our future correspondence might have been cordial and even fruitful, but not of the same existential urgency. So for those who see this as the beginning of what might have been a beautiful relationship, my guess is, probably not.

One concluding footnote on the paintings that are mentioned in the later letters. These were kind of black ink Zen brush drawings that Merton had done. He was concerned that they not be exploited commercially and asked me to get them. I did so and felt it a significant expression of the trust that he felt toward me that he gave me this task. When he died I was left holding these drawings. Feeling committed to carry out his request that they not be exploited commercially, but used for some social good, I used most of them for an auction to raise money for the Berrigan Defense Fund that was defending Dan and Phil Berrigan against an absurd U.S. government effort to indict them on conspiracy charges. This seemed like the sort of cause that would be appropriate to Merton's intentions.

I have no idea where these paintings have landed today. In my ascetic feelings of non-commercialism, I made no effort to keep track of those who purchased them in this process of raising money for the Berrigans' defense. I have only one picture, which I kept and which I reproduce for this collection of letters.

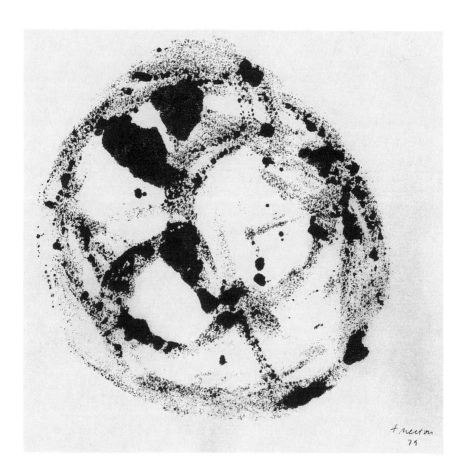

THE LETTERS

August 12, 1966

Dear Father Louis:

*J*ustus Lawler [editor at Herder and Herder] passed on your recent letter to me with your very kind remarks on my article. He indicated to me that you might be interested in seeing the manuscript I have finished preparing entitled "The Church Against Herself," of which the Vahanian article forms one Chapter.[1] At present I have only my personal carbon copy, somewhat the worn for wear for having been read on the beach with Fr. Berrigan and several IHM novices. I would be happy to send it on to you, however, if you were interested and could return it sometime toward the end of September, when I expect proofs from the publisher should be coming through.

I recently had a letter from Fr. Robert Adolfs, OSA of Holland, who described a recently completed manuscript of his, *The Grave of God* (the "grave" = the church!!), which sounded much like the ideas I have been struggling with. He also was very enthusiastic about the Vahanian article and remarked that he wished he had written it himself!!

Yours in the Baseleia tou Theou,
[Reign of God]

Rosemary

❧

August 18, 1966

Dear Rosemary:

I do very much want to read your book, but there are several reasons why it would probably not be too good an idea to

---

1. Rosemary Ruether, "Vahanian: The Worldly Church and the Churchly World," *Continuum* 4, no. 1 (Spring 1966): 50–62.

send your only carbon. First of all, things tend to get lost around here. Second, I am going to be hung up in various ways for the next few weeks and probably would not be able to get to it easily. Probably, it would be better if I could get a set of proofs. Who is doing the book, Herder? They probably would not mind. On the other hand, this does not mean that I would necessarily be able to promise a preface. (I have to ration the prefaces almost out of existence these days.) But if the Vahanian piece is any indication, I think you have an extraordinary book going. Glad the Dutch Father is so enthusiastic. It is absolutely necessary to do something about the pseudo-optimism that is floating around and is only the old static triumphalism in a new costume.

Vahanian is one man I must read. I have been reading a bit of [Thomas J.] Altizer, whom I respect, and [William] Hamilton, who is touchingly naive and sometimes just plain stupid — but I felt very sympathetic to him in an essay called "Thursday's Child."[2] Glad you saw Dan out there: he wrote a couple of very good letters from the Coast.

Do let me know about the proofs — or I could read the carbon when you have less need of it.

You might be interested in this article — part of a series for a Brazilian newspaper.[3] I represent our team, with Toynbee, Radakrishnan, and so on, batting for other sides. It is elementary and safe, I suppose. But perhaps it suggests some right directions. I would be happy if you would send along anything that you think would be good for me to read, I depend to a great extent on the light and love of my friends who keep me informed, notified, alerted, etc.

> With my best wishes, in Christ,
> *Tom*

---

2. Thomas J. Altizer and William Hamilton were known as "Death of God" theologians.

3. Thomas Merton, "Christian Humanism," *Jornal do Brasil*. Also published in English in *Love and Living* (New York: Farrar, Straus & Giroux, 1979).

Late August/Early September 1966

Dear Father Louis:

*T*he carbon of my book has currently strayed out of my hands into those of a graduate student at the University of Chicago. I expect it back in a few weeks. Lawler has another and the London people the original. So I expect the proofs would be best. Questions of preface I leave up to Lawler. Sheed and Ward, London, I believe have gotten the consent of Fr. Adolfs to do a preface for the European edition and are already working on foreign translations, but I think Lawler wants someone stateside for US edition, as he thinks Fr. Adolfs is not well enough known here.

I was glancing over your humanism article and noticed your remarks about Renaissance Popes and Galileo. I wonder if that would have happened one hundred years earlier. The post-Trentine Popes were both more "virtuous" and less kindly than those who reigned in an earlier, looser age. The mistresses of Alexander VI are well known, but who remembers that he freed Pico della Mirandola from the prison into which an inquisitorial type had thrown him and sent him back to Florence with admonitions to be a good boy. One hundred years later Pico would have been burned.

A few other comments: "Transform evil into good"? That can lead to an easy theodicy. Let's just say, forgive an evil which remains none the less evil. I think you would enjoy reading more of Bonhoeffer, if you are not already well acquainted with him. He explicitly develops the relationship of narcissism and original sin (identity rather), i.e., *Act and Being*. My own thought is increasingly informed by Bonhoeffer, and indeed the Lutheran form of theologizing generally strikes me as a more mature Christianity than either the old triumphalism or the new optimism and naturalism of Catholicism.

I send along a carbon of a little essay closely related to these topics which I recently sent to *Commonweal*.[4] I don't know if they will take it. They are fearfully cliquish and don't cotton to characters like myself who do not admire the club. The stress on the eschatological pole and the description of man "in the middle" seems to me an essential way to overcome a certain type of undialectical incarnationalism which rapidly ceases to take sin seriously and must unhistorically overlook the reality of what man's existence really is (and that means in the church, nay rather, *as* the church).

I don't know whether you have read Dan Sullivan's recent sexual mysticism. I read his latest piece in *Commonweal*[5] as I was leaving California and surveying the rubble of most of our friends' marriages. As our various friends came to cry on my shoulder and pour out their frustrations against the other, it became obvious that these relationships were built on exploitation from the beginning. That was when I decided to champion the new heresy of Augustinianism against the new Sullivanesque orthodoxy of the Catholic liberal establishment.

I am gradually becoming rather anti-Teilhardian as well. Partly because the new sort of Catholic Hegelians take him up and use the most dubious aspect of his work, and, secondly, because it seems to me that he too shares some of this great theodicy which makes evil simply the shadows on a great masterpiece and so again loses the Christian seriousness of man's perversity, has no sense of radical evil and, so ultimately, becomes rather inhuman; check his comments on the exploding of the atom bomb for example. To Teilhard it is all a magnificent release of

---

4. Later published as Rosemary Ruether, "A Query to Daniel Sullivan: Bonhoeffer on Sexuality," *Continuum* 4, no. 3 (Autumn 1966): 457–60.

5. Dan Sullivan, "Letter to the Editors," *Commonweal* 84, no. 23 (September 30, 1966): 649.

energy. The only accurate description of man, it seems to me, is the one Bonhoeffer developed: "Man in the middle" alienated from his beginning, glimpsing his end only in faith and hope, i.e., *theologia crucis*. It is this stance which seems to me to define a position over against both old Catholic triumphalism and new Catholic liberalism, i.e., an anti-liberal Christian radicalism.

Speaking of radicals, I am so concerned about my friend Bill DuBay.[6] He is now treading very near the abyss. Before I left California, I wrote him urging him not to fight the establishment, but to ignore it, above all not to sue McIntyre in the civil courts which is his great scheme. To do this means money, and the money for such a thing would come from POU types [Protestants and Others United for Separation of Church and State]; such allies would be the final unforgiveable sin. Yet, I wonder if I was right. DuBay wants to be the sacrificial lamb, hurling himself against the evil institution, testing its assumptions and false justice in the courts. Since he wants to destroy himself for the sake of our salvation, maybe we should let him and see what happens. Please give me your reaction to this situation. I am quite in two minds about which course he should take, and I know very well that any advice to back down or submit, for him, would be a prostitution of his conscience. Maybe someone has to test the system all the way to the last extremity, and Bill is certainly willing to do just that. In fact he now seems to live for nothing else. I fear he will destroy his soul in the process, however. I don't see in him some calm centre of spirituality which can stand above the storm. His whole self is totally immanent in the fight. He really needs our love, I hope you don't mind if I ask you these questions. I, too, depend on people

---

6. Father William DuBay of the Los Angeles archdiocese had requested that the pope remove the cardinal of that archdiocese, James Francis McIntyre. The basis of his request was the cardinal's repression of all involvement in civil rights by diocesan priests and religious. See Rosemary Ruether, "Crisis in Los Angeles," *Continuum* 2, no. 4 (Winter 1965): 652–62.

with special insights to "beat sword against shield and rescue the holy sparks."

Best,
Rosemary Ruether

September 21, 1966

Dear Rosemary:

*T*hanks for your letter and for the essay on the Augustinian theology of sexuality which I liked very much. I don't know Bonhoeffer's *Act and Being*. I have read his *Ethics* and Prison Letters and have quoted the former here and there in my new book [*Conjectures of a Guilty Bystander*], of which I will send you a copy. It is rather a mish mash, but there may be things in it that you will like. Certainly you will find me liking Bonhoeffer. Did your essay make the *Commonweal?* I don't get it now, so I don't know exactly what Daniel Sullivan could have been saying. (Don't know him. Know a Dan Callahan. They sound alike.) The point you make about accepting the man-woman relation as a true acceptance of createdness is very necessary. That this is a relationship of limit and not of fusion. I think though there is also the ecstatic element in the Augustinian tradition on love that can be emphasized too. Ecstasy is not fusion but the perfection of giving, *caritas*. Fusion, narcissism, are on the level of *cupiditas*. You bring this out well. There is a lot there, and I am all for you. I think as you do that this naive optimistic naturalism only trivializes sex and adds to the speed with which it becomes impossible for people to cope with. (Some sentence that.) I haven't really read much Teilhard since an article of mine on the *Divine Milieu* was not allowed to be published by the censors of the Order. (Teilhard too wicked.) I was not sufficiently concerned to read

– 8 –

him when I couldn't do anything with it — I'm not sold enough on him to read it for pure illumination and uplift. So I didn't read him.

Bill DuBay answered a sort of concerned letter I had sent him. He is very sure of himself. He knows his cause is right and therefore. . . . But it is not enough just to be "in the right." That does not authorize one to forget all other considerations. My impression is that he is not going to listen to advice that does not go along the lines that he has decided to take, and these are leading to a collision course that at the best will result in his being a victim for everyone. Will it do any good? The point I was trying to make was that he was not really communicating anything clear, either to the hierarchy or to the rest of us. He was just being dramatic. I don't think he accepted any of that at all. He exhorted me to embrace "radical honesty" and that settled it as far as he was concerned. Evidently to suggest going slow is conservative dishonesty.

I very much liked your essay. Do please keep in touch and send along any more ideas like these. I am returning it, supposing you need every copy you can lay hands on.

All the best always in Christ,
Tom Merton

❦

October 10, 1966

Dear Father Merton:

*M*any thanks for your book which arrived today. I was poking through it here and there. I think your perspective is much like mine, although with a little more touch of melancholia where I tend to be angry, also without the agonizing I have done over modern Bible exegesis which makes it so difficult to make the kind of statements about "what the church teaches" which still come easily to you. It is precisely this agony which I seem to share with so few other Catholics (except perhaps Küng who struggles with this too), and makes me feel so apart from them. They take for granted things which for me are not only questionable, but insupportable.

I am teaching a church history class at George Washington, a large street car secular college. I enjoy the type of student there, serious yet unpretentious (unlike hothouse academia), sharply critical yet not pretentiously carping either (again unlike hothouse academia). These are students who are usually paying their own way, not being supported by their parents, and they can't afford to waste time with certain kinds of pretensions that the ivy league type can afford to play with. I had one student in my class, a freshman, rigidly schooled Catholic, product of the Benedictine Priory. He wanted to play it unsafe by not going to Catholic college, but coming to GW. But he came in fear and trembling, sure that his faith would be in jeopardy every step of the way. He was assured that "he would get a Catholic" for his church history course. Poor advice!! My first two lectures covering the preaching of Jesus and the early *kerygma* were apparently the most traumatic experience of his life. He was in literal agony. He felt he should go on, but confessed to me that it took him hours to read a few pages of the assigned reading; the revelations contained therein (merely Williston Walker's standard church history by the way) were so horrendous to his presuppositions. He finally decided to drop, he wasn't ready to hear such things (not that he thought they were untrue, mind you, but just that he wasn't ready to hear such things). When is this gap going to close!! When are our schools going to stop preparing people for some other world and making them unfit to deal with this one??? He wants to keep on talking to me, nevertheless. He said he felt he must get more background before he could take such a course. I felt like suggesting that he might get more background by taking a church history course, mine for example, but I knew what he meant even if it did not make "logical" sense. So there you are. I went through the same thing as a college student. I survived. I find the whole picture of the real Christianity infinitely more "real" than the mythical one. Yet must I force him through the same crucifixion; such an unnecessary crucifixion, an old aeon created by the church herself, which must be put to death again and again in every new generation, who then conclude by this (quite logically) that the church which lives in such a mythical world is a church which they must leave in order to come of age?

Then there are those who stay and fight, but again so naively, so unprepared theologically for such a fight — they turn stupid and fanatic (embrace radical honesty indeed!!). It would be better if they got out. I feel such a terrible build up of wrath over the church; it really makes me shudder to go near the inner Catholic world, so I hang on the fringes, usually celebrate with Protestants, etc. I can't do the transformation bit — there is no presto change here, no changing of wrath into love — I love the church, but that doesn't do anything to alter the dimensions of this wrath, but rather intensifies it to the limit.

Best,

Rosemary

P.S. Dan Sullivan and Dan Callahan are not the same, but very different indeed. Enclose clipping.[7]

✽✽✽

---

7. Ruether sent Merton a copy of Sullivan's "Letter to the Editors"; see footnote 5 above. This letter is a critique of Callahan's article "Religious Slum-Dwellers," published August 19 in *Commonweal*.

Dear Friends:[8]

Several wrote that they liked my mimeographed Christmas letter and urged me to go on mimeographing more often. This has one advantage: at least I can send replies to letters which I could not otherwise be able to answer. I am once again forced to keep down letters to a minimum. First of all, Lent is close — Easter is early this year. Then, my publisher fondly imagines that I am working on a book for which I have signed a contract, so I had better get busy on it. For three months I have not been able to do anything with this manuscript because I have been bombarded with requests for other things — articles, statements, and so on, plus correspondence. Now I want to concentrate on my true work for a while. And of course live my life. Hence, another mimeograph. I hope those who did not know about this, and who expected a personal reply, will have the kindness to understand.

It is a quiet, cloudy Sunday morning, not too cold. I am hoping for some rain to fill my rain barrels and give me water to wash dishes with. I still have enough to wash out the coffee pot for another three or four days. I bring drinking water daily from the monastery in a gallon bottle. I know what it means to save on water, and I guess I use only two or three gallons a day for everything at the hermitage. (Showers I take at the monastery.)

There has been a lot of talk about Fr. Charles Davis and his farewell to the Church. Note, his problem was Church authority, not celibacy. He could conceivably have left the priesthood and gotten married with a dispensation. In a long statement, which was front page news in England, he made some very drastic criticisms of the abuse of authority in the Church. I

---

8. This letter, though not a personal letter to Ruether, is included as part of the correspondence because Merton makes reference to it in another letter to Ruether; it also offers a unique historical contextualization through its discussion of Charles Davis.

do not think these criticisms were altogether baseless or unjust. The present institutional structure of the Church is certainly too antiquated, too baroque, and is often in practice unjust, inhuman, arbitrary, and even absurd in its functioning. It sometimes imposes useless and intolerable burdens on the human person and demands outrageous sacrifices, often with no better result than to maintain a rigid system in its rigidity and to keep the same abuses established, one might think, until kingdom come. I certainly respect Fr. Davis's anguish — who of us does not sometimes share it? But I cannot follow him in his conclusion that the institutional Church has now reached the point where it can hardly be anything other than dishonest, tyrannical, mendacious, and inhuman. He feels he has a moral obligation to leave the Church, and he offers this theological justification for his decision.

I hope most of us Catholics have learned by now that this kind of decision on the part of one of our brothers, merits our compassion and understanding, not fulminations against heresy and bad faith. One can feel Fr. Davis is still a brother without coming to the same conclusions as he did.

I have, in fact, just been reading Romano Guardini's excellent little book on Pascal. He analyzes the "demon of combativeness" in Pascal — a demon which is no prerogative of Jansenists. At times one wonders if a certain combativeness is not endemic in Catholicism: a "compulsion to be always right" and to prove the adversary wrong. A compulsion which easily leads to witch hunting and which, when turned the wrong way, hunts its witches in the Church herself and finally needs to find them in Rome. There are always human failures which can be exploited for this purpose. Pascal nearly went over the falls completely, but he recognized the destructiveness of his own inner demon in time, and knew enough to be silent and to believe and to love. The story of his death is very moving.

There comes a time when it is no longer important to prove one's point, but simply to live, to surrender to God and to love.

There have been bad days when I might have considered doing what Fr. Davis has done. In actual fact, I have never seriously considered leaving the Church, and though the question of leaving the monastic state *has* presented itself, I was not able to take it seriously for more than five or ten minutes. It is true that if I had at one time or another left the Church, I would have found scores of friends who would have approved my action and declared it honest and courageous. I do not claim any special merit in having decided otherwise. Nor does a decision for Christian obedience imply an admission that I think authority has always been infallibly just, reasonable, or human. Being a Catholic and being a monk have not always been easy. But I know that I owe too much to the Church and to Christ for me to be able to take these other things seriously. The absurdity, the prejudice, the rigidity, and unreasonableness one encounters in some Catholics are nothing whatever when placed in the balance with the grace, love, and infinite mercy of Christ in His Church. And after all, am I not arrogant too? Am I not unreasonable, unfair, demanding, suspicious, and often quite arbitrary in my dealings with others? The point is not just "who is right?" but "judge not" and "forgive one another" and "bear one another's burdens." This by no means implies passive obsequiousness and blind obedience, but a willingness to listen, to be patient, and to keep working to help the Church change and renew herself from within. This is our task. Therefore, by God's grace I remain a Catholic, a monk and a hermit. I have made commitments which are unconditional and cannot be taken back. I do not regard this position as especially courageous: it is just the ordinary stuff of life, the acceptance of limits which we must all accept in one way or another: the acceptance of a sphere in which one is called to love, trust, and believe, and pray — and meet those whom one is destined to meet and love.

More and more I see the meaning of my relationship with all of you, and the value of the love that unites us, usually unexpressed. This is the area in which the term "union in Christ" really means most to me, though some of you are not enrolled in my Church.

More and more, since living alone, I have wanted to stop fighting, and arguing, and proclaiming, and criticizing. I think the points on which protest has been demanded of me and given by me are now well enough known. Obviously, there may be other such situations in the future. In a world like ours — a world of war, riot, murder, racism, tyranny and established banditry, one has to be able to stand up and say NO. But there are also other things to do. I am more and more convinced of the reality of my own job, which is meditation and study and prayer in silence. I do not intend to give up writing, that too is obviously my vocation. But I hope I will be able to give up controversy some day. Pray for me. When one gets older (Jan. 31 is my fifty-second birthday) one realizes the futility of a life wasted in argument when it should be given entirely to love.

God bless you. I really appreciate your letters. When there are really urgent questions and problems in them, I will always do my level best to answer. Please understand that my visits are severely limited, and I cannot possibly even think of seeing more than a few people who ask to see me. But there is such a thing as being united in prayer, or even thought and desire (if you can't pray) and in our friendship. The main thing is that we desire good for each other and seek, within the limits of our power, to obtain for each other what we desire.

Cordially yours in Christ,
Thomas Merton

P.S. For those who have not been in touch with developments here: I have been living, more or less, as a hermit for several years. The dividing line between "less" and "more" came in the Fall of 1964 when I began spending the night in the hermitage. Living there day and night became "official" in August 1965. My latest book: *Conjectures of a Guilty Bystander* (Doubleday — November 1966). The next one *Mystics and Zen Masters* (Farrar, Straus and

Giroux — March 1967). New Directions will publish two paper-
backs of mine in 1967 — a new *Selected Poems* and *Wisdom of the
Desert.*

※

Dear Rosemary:

I have been thinking of this letter for a while, and so I am
writing it. The immediate occasion: the discussion on woman
in the *Commonweal.*[9] Not that I want to add anything to that. I
thought your points were very good and those of Sr. Aloysius too.
The whole question is terribly important, but I don't know where
to begin on that so I'll keep quiet. Yet in a way the letter has
oblique reference to the question because it happens that you, a
woman, are for some reason a theologian I trust. Almost the only
one. And I do think I need the help of a theologian. Do you think
you could help me once in a while? I do not intend to be very demanding on your time, but I would like to feel that I can resort
to you for suggestions and advice. Not so much for my work, as
just to help me think. I have no great project in mind. I just need
help in two areas where I have serious trouble and where I have
simply been avoiding a confrontation: the Bible and the Church.

To begin with the Church: I have no problem about "leaving"
or anything. My problem with "authority" is just the usual one,
and I can survive it. But the real Church. I am simply browned
off with and afraid of Catholics. All Catholics, from Ottaviani to
DuBay, all down the damn line. There are a few Catholics I can
stand with equanimity when I forget they are Catholics and remember they are just my friends, like Dan Berrigan and Ed Rice
and Sister Mary Luke and a lot of people like that. I love the

---

9. Rosemary Ruether, "The Woman Intellectual and the Church," symposium in
Commonweal 85, no. 16 (January 27, 1967): 446–58.

monks, but they might as well be in China. I love all the nice well-meaning good people who go to Mass and want things to get better and so on, but I understand Zen Buddhists better than I do them, and the Zens understand me better. But this is awful because where is the Church, and where am I in the Church? You are a person who might have an idea of the Church that might help me and that I might trust. An idea of the Church in which projects and crusades (ancient or modern) or ideas (new or old) or policies or orthodoxies (old or new) don't stand in the way between people. Is the Church a community of people who love each other or a big dog fight where you do your religious business seeking, meanwhile, your friends somewhere else?

Could you suggest something good on this? I haven't been reading Catholic stuff, books or magazines, for a long time (except recently Guardini on Pascal). I'd be perfectly content to forget I am a Catholic. I suppose that is bad faith, because meanwhile I continue in a monastery and a hermitage where I am content with life, and the institution is supporting me in this. I just want to have as little as possible to do with the parades and the acclamations.

As to the Bible, I read it in peace and fruitlessly I suppose. I don't try to follow the new stuff about it because there is just too much. But I ought to. And since you have mentioned that a couple of times, I wish you would recommend something.

I know this is a pretty bad letter (guilt about saying all this). But I do wonder at times if the Church is real at all. I believe it, you know. But I wonder if I am nuts to do so. Am I part of a great big hoax? I don't explain myself as well as I would like to: there is a real sense of and confidence in an underlying reality, the presence of Christ in the world which I don't doubt for an instant. But is that presence where we are all saying it is? We are all pointing (in various directions), and my dreadful feeling is that we are all pointing wrong. Could you point someplace for me, maybe?

The enclosed says a little more of the same...

Thanks, and I am sorry to bother you. I have to write a book on monasticism, and I wonder if I can make it relevant — or make any sense with it at all. (I have no problem with my vocation).

In His love,
Tom

﷽

February 1967

Dear Thomas Merton:

I was profoundly moved by your last letter. I have had a feeling in reading your words previously that you were holding back: that though you were treating profound ideas, you were doing it with the surface depth of your being. In this letter I felt some swirl of deeper troubled waters that I had sensed were being held back, but I didn't expect to see them surface. I thought that the "Catholic" structure would keep them under. It is almost impossible for me to do anything but make some gesture of reply since I only see some distant smoke rising, and don't even know the whole aetiology of the fire, nor would I even want to, since ultimately this most basic level has to be dealt with by each person in terrible loneliness. It is almost indecent to invade this sanctuary. Perhaps that is why I have always been slightly repelled by the Catholic "spiritual director" bit. We speak in a kind of hieroglyphics to each other, and when real contact is made, it is not some immediacy to each other that is best, but authenticity on each of our parts and leaving it to the Holy Spirit to decode the message, to transform our word into a Word of God for our fellows. We never know when that will happen. Our best efforts may do nothing for someone else, and then some chance remark may be the "moment of truth."

I am sending you my manuscript very much worn.[10] It is a very labyrinthine set of hieroglyphics and none of it may speak to your situation, but it is my gesture of what I can say about these things, i.e., the Bible and the Church, insofar as I have been able to work out these same problems in my own mind and for my own existence.

Let me just try to kind of make some "brief formulas," to use Plato's phrase, to catch those two things about which you asked:

The Church: What it is; surely not first of all the institution. This structure blasphemes when it says it was founded by Christ. It was not founded by Christ, but by history; as such it is a necessary but secondary structure serving as the temporal vehicle for a tradition about a certain reality; but that reality is not only, or even primarily, happening there. That reality is nothing else but God's constant renewal of His good creation, which has fallen into alienation and estrangement. The Church as historical vehicle carries the words about this good news, but in its own substance exhibits more deeply than anywhere else this fallenness and estrangement which is the condition from which God is saving his creation. The "true church" is wherever this reality is happening, and it is to the glory of God's omnipotence that this reality is now beginning to happen a little bit, here and there, in the structure which we must so misleadingly call the "church."

The Bible: This problem is part and parcel with our wrong definition of God's incarnation. God's incarnation is not a magical new nature — this is the heresy which was condemned as monophysitism, but which we have never been able to purge out of our hellenistic souls. Incarnation, whether Jesus, the Bible, the Church, the Eucharist — this is man's word about God's Word — as God's Word it is really God-with-us. But this happens within or rather *as* words, persons, gestures, "stuff" that itself remains quite human, fallible, stumbling, imperfect, full of error and sin.

---

10. Rosemary Ruether, *The Church against Itself* (New York: Herder and Herder, 1967).

Once we get this proper relation of man's word to God's Word straight (which ultimately means rethinking Christology all over again), then the Bible, the historical Jesus will cease to scandalize us, not to mention church history. I think, for a Catholic, Loisy is a good person to read — his last two books on the development of the Christian tradition. If a Catholic can accept this (granted some attitudes are outdated, but the scholarship has held up remarkably well) he is ready to accept the humanity of God's Word.

You say that you have no trouble with your vocation, but, if that is really true, maybe you should be having some trouble with your vocation. I love the monastic life dearly (I am a Third Order Benedictine) but today it is no longer the eschatological sign and witness in the church. For those who wish to be at the "kingdom" frontier of history, it is the steaming ghetto of the big city, not the countryside that is the place of the radical overcoming of this world, the place where one renews creation, disposes of oneself and does hand to hand combat with the demons. I don't see how anyone who is stuck in the old moribund (once eschatological) structures and is at the same time alive to the times cannot be having some trouble with his vocation. But perhaps for you more important: mere more *reading* and *thinking* about Word and Church will not help. I think you will have to find some new way of having Word and Church happening *for you*. Perhaps you have gone as far as you can go in the hermitage direction; you are running out of fat from previously accumulated community contact, and need renewal in a period of service. I may be wrong, may be operating on *a priori* prejudice, and if so, forgive. But that is what I saw rising between the lines, a cry of help for community — "I have no trouble with my vocation"(?) the hermit doth protest too much. Withdrawal and solitude is not a life vocation; it is part of a larger rhythm of life. One needs to return to the cave to help those imprisoned therein, else one's contemplation remains sterile; indeed I wonder if one can even contemplate out of relation of touch, sight, smell, verbal feel of one another. The face of God is revealed in the face of our brother.

As for Catholics, surely we must rescue the word Catholic like the word church from its false captivity. To the extent that we are Romans we are less "Catholic." I find very little in "Roman" thought that helps my thought. I keep up with it to see how "we" (the retarded child, the angry adolescent) are "coming along," but when I want prophetic insight I look to Barth, Bonhoeffer, Bultmann, etc. I wonder if the "browned off" with catholics isn't a passé question, like Davis' reasons for leaving the church, an absolutizing of a relative cultural style which we are already surpassing. Perhaps the deeper question for you which you may not be really taking into account is whether you really want to be a Christian or not, whether you want to be an authentically creational, incarnate flesh and blood man, or whether you want to be an abstraction, zen mystic. I feel the shreds tying you to the Judeo-Christian sense of life a bit raveling out. Again maybe I am prejudiced. Also I think we all write too much, we have to fight off these bloody publishers who want us to contract for things we are not really writing.

I hope that some of this is or may be helpful.

> Charis emin kai eirene,
> [Grace to us and peace]
> *Rosemary*

❀

February 14, 1967

Dear Rosemary:

*M*any thanks for your very good letter. It was what I needed, a sign that someone was there and that my own struggle with the institution was not madness, hubris or something. I do see, as you do, how demonic it can be. Your manuscript is fine on that. I agree with you all along about the hardening of the Church as institution and idol and its becoming against what it ought to be a sign of. If we and others see this problem — and it is pretty terrible — then there *is* something going on, anyway, and if there is smoke going up here and there that is something. I also think we will be a very scattered Church for a while. But as long as I know what direction seems to be the one to go in, I will gladly go in it.

So, in your book first of all: what you say about the Church as happening clicks perfectly. I think what I really wanted to know most of all was that my own personal "sense" of when Church happens was not just self-deception — at least not purely so. Because if that is where God speaks and the Spirit acts, then I can be confident that God has not abandoned us. Not left us at the mercy of the princes of the Church. Unless we insist on being trampled by them.

What I don't know about is the Christology. I am not arguing about it. It is just that my coming into the Church was marked by a pretty strong and dazzled belief in the Christ of the Nicene Creed. One reason for this was a strong reaction against the fogginess and subjectivity and messed-up-ness of the ideas about Christ that I had met with up and down in various types of Protestantism. I was tired of a Christ who had evaporated. But that is not what is bugging me, and I will see about it all if I get to reading Loisy. What does bother me theologically (I am not enough of a theologian to be really bothered by theological problems) is the sense that when you go into the history of the Church you run into a bigger and bigger hole of unconscious bad faith, and, at that point, I get rather uneasy about our dictating to all the "other religions" that we are the one authentic outfit that has the real goods. I am not saying that I want to be able to mix Christianity and Buddhism in quantities to suit myself, however. Far from it. I think you got me wrong on that. Please tip me off if something new and good shows up on Incarnation.

About monasticism, my vocation and all that. I made too much of a shorthand statement there. I always tend to assume that everyone knows I have had a monumental struggle with monasticism as it now is and still disagree violently with most of the party line policies. I am a notorious maverick in the Order, and my Abbot considers me a dangerous subject always ready to run off with a woman or something, so I am under constant surveillance. If I am allowed to live in a hermitage, it is theoretically because this will keep me more under wraps than otherwise. So when I say I "have no problem with my vocation," I just mean that I am not, for the moment, standing over the Abbot with a smoking gun in my hand. In other words, I have the usual agonia with my vocation, but now, after twenty-five years, I am in a position where I am practically laicized and de-institutionalized and living like all the other old bats who live alone in the hills in this part of the country, and I feel like a human being again. My hermit life is expressly a *lay* life. I never wear the habit except when at the monastery, and I try to be as much on my own as I can and like the people around in the country. Also, I try as best I can to keep up valid and living contacts with my friends who are in the thick of things, and everyone knows where my real "community" is. I honestly believe that this is the right place for me (woods, not Gethsemani) in so far as it is the right battleground. It is a sort of guerilla-outpost type of thing if you like. But from my experience I would myself be leading a less honest and more faked life if I were back in the cities. This isn't a reflection on anyone else. In staying here I am not just being here for myself but for my friends, my Church, and all those I am one with. Also, if there is one thing I am sure of, it is my need to fight out in my own heart whatever sort of fight for honesty I have to wage and for fidelity to God. I am not by any means turning my back on other people; I am as open as the situation (of overcontrol) permits and want to make this more open as time goes on. Lots of people would like me to get out and join them in this or that, but I just don't see that I could do it without getting into some absurd role and having to act a part or justify some nonsense or other that I don't really believe in. I know I firmly disbelieve all the favorite clichés about monasticism, and the community knows it too. I can't say where or how my life is eschatological, because as far as I can see I am a tramp and not much else. But this kind of tramp is what I am supposed to be. This kind of place is where I am finally reduced to my nothingness and have to depend on God. Outside I would be much more able to depend on talk. Maybe I am just protesting too much, but that is the way I feel about it. I assure you that whatever else it is it is not complacency, because there is ample material for not being complacent, I assure you.

This is really too much, but thanks, anyway, for your good letter and your manuscript which I am returning. I really do see things very much your way and will have to read Vahanian and more of Bonhoeffer. About Zen: not abstract at all the way I see it. I use it for idol cracking and things like that. Healthy way of keeping one's house clean. Gets the dust out quicker than anything I know. I am not talking about purity, just breathing, and not piling up the mental junk. Thanks again.

Peace in His love,
Tom Merton

P.S. I do very much appreciate your good words, and I feel we are striving for the same thing though in very different ways. Our contact can be fruitful, I think, for badly needed monastic renewal. So much to be done there! I am sending some inadequate notes on that and can send more.

One of my real problems with the Institution is that, in the name of monastic solitude, I am forbidden to participate in conferences, etc., which are an obvious necessity at this time. This is a real deviation and perversion in the mind of the Superior concerned (who imagines himself inspired by the Holy Spirit!!). This *is* a problem of vocation. I'll have to meet it one of these days.

Dear Thomas Merton:

I was relieved to get your sane letter. I tend to write missives without realizing it and then afterwards really worry if the poor guy has been trampled to death. I didn't know if there was some big thing that you really were hiding from yourself and that maybe I had kicked it open in some way that would just undercut and not save, but I should have had more faith in your self-knowledge. I think the inner-city jazz is the biggest place of self-delusion in a way, although it is the self-delusion of petty schemes and grandiose dreams, while suburbia is just the delusion of insomnia. But I tend to be afraid of these woods because when I am out there doing the big ingathering and contemplating bit I get all caught up in rising ecstasy of communing with God and then discover I have been communing with nothing but myself. This drives me back to the absolute necessity for prophetic community which can really strip us open and be the place of revelation for us, standing concretely for the "otherness" of God which I never seem to get except in encounter with others, never in self contemplation, but then you know more about that.

I distrust all academic theology. Only theology bred in the crucible of experience is any good. I like Vahanian on incarnation. He speaks of an incarnation I can make contact with, whereas Catholic incarnationalism seems always to be quasi-docetic, and metahistorical. The agony of plain history has dismantled that Catholic Christ for me bit by bit until finally the last fragment of it is gone, and I am relieved. Jesus was a Jewish eschatological prophet filled with visions of the kingdom of God, increasingly convinced that he was God's instrument to announce the crucial hour; he and his disciples went up to Jerusalem to see the great glory, and he got strung up like a common criminal, and his followers cut the scene like rabbits. What then to do? Admit you were just wrong, or quixotically reaffirm the vision in a new form? Turn the denouement itself into salvation? Something like that. All very human, and yet revelation, the start of a seminal idea that continually lights up reality in new ways. But basically this salvation is not some magic figure in the past, but the disclosure situation here and now for me, the Christological structure of creation of which Jesus of Nazareth is historically the foundational *kairos* [critical moment or crucial time in history], but which we encounter not by encountering that one but this one right here before me. The article on ministry as encounter is my Christology.[11] I am hung up on writing books too. Herder and Herder want me to do something on radical theology; somebody else wants me to do something on development of doctrine. I, like a dope, make hopeful noises to these people instead of just saying: "I will write a book when I write it, and when I have one written, you can see it." More and more I am moved to do a *Jesu-buch.* It seems to me that a good analysis of this whole historical Jesus/Christ of faith is what needs to be clarified more than anything else. Although I may end up being the Catholic D. F. Strauss. Catholics, I have a feeling, are more afraid of that than anything else. That is the linch pin of their whole idolatry. Protestants at least know better, but don't want to admit what it is and so get very tricky and obscure; only a cryptographist could figure out what they are saying. If I were you I would look at the plain New Testament historians like Dibelius and Stendahl, not Bultmann and those who are trying to simultaneously create a new theology. Try to get the picture: *was eigenlich gewesen war* [what actually happened] clearly, and then test the theologies in that crucible. Maybe Loisy is only fun after you have had a long training in that, because he is bitter and polemical and that throws things off. I wish that he was still alive, I would write him appreciation letters. Did you know that as an ex-communicate he was constantly harassed, barbers wouldn't cut his hair? The old taboo psychology.

---

11. Rosemary Ruether, "Ministry in the Church of the Future," in Gerald Sloyan, ed., *Secular Priest in the New Church* (New York: Herder and Herder, 1967), 232–49.

I hope things haven't gotten that bad down on the farm!! I am really sorry to hear of misunderstanding. I thought maybe everyone was just wrapped in daydreams, not suspicions as well. My dear friend Father Vincent Martin of St. Andrew's Priory, Valyermo, took that for a long time from his Prior and was finally shoved out. A very cruel thing that opened my eyes to the petty lovelessness that can go on among monastic brothers. That's what comes of thinking you are "out of this world."

It is a good thing we believe in a Jewish God who has a good sense of humor!!

Love,
Rosemary

P.S. You will have to teach me better about Zen. I have tried to read some, and probably am less interested because of the S. F. [San Francisco] Alan Watts crowd which seemed to be getting more degenerate every day. Zen, and Eastern thought in general, seems so impoverished to me compared to the richness of the Christian mythos, basically the lack of the sense of creation.

The enclosed from 3 year old Mimi.[12]

※※

Early March 1967

Dear Thomas Merton:

*W*hat can I say about your paper on monastic renewal?? Let us just admit at the outset that I am radically out of sympathy with the monastic project, not merely in its fallen state, but also in its original and most intrinsic self-understanding. This being the case, I despair of being able to say anything useful to you. But maybe I can at least explain my divergence. Monasticism

---

12. Christmas card showing Ruether's daughter Mimi in a protest march with a sign saying, "War is unhealthy for children and other living things."

represents a total view of what salvation means, what it means to overcome the world and bring in the kingdom of God. It is nothing at all if it cannot make the most radical claim for this point of view, if it cannot claim that this and this alone is the way to be Christian, that only monks are fully Christian and all others are members of the "half-way covenant." Therefore, it seems to me, that faced with this claim, one cannot equivocate. One cannot say, well, that is all right for you but not for me, but we both are equally good Christians. You like your woods, I like my city, and so forth. Either monasticism is the fullness of the gospel, or else it has lost its authentic rationale and lives on as a fossil of its former self. The fact is that Christianity has almost totally rejected that rationale. Even monks themselves scarcely dare to claim that they, and only they, are fully Christian and that all who really take the gospel seriously must necessarily become monks. This claim, I propose to you, is now rejected not merely by those who don't want to take the gospel seriously, but precisely by those who today wish to be radical Christians. And thus monasticism, no longer today standing for radical Christianity, has indeed lost its soul, and the question which you asked at the outset of the paper, "whether we believe that there is a way for modern men to be monks in a new way," is really the crucial question and the question that I would answer in the negative. Having said this, I must then go on to be consistent enough to suggest that monasticism, not only today, but always was a misunderstanding of the gospel, and the dichotomies of monastic life have ever revealed this fact. Namely, that salvation is precisely salvation *of* and not *from* the world. No one who takes this proposition seriously can consider monasticism as the true expression of a radical Christianity, because monasticism, no matter how much it tempers its language and mixes itself up in "openness" to the world, is rooted in a view of the gospel that makes salvation a salvation *from* the world and not the salvation *of* the world. The point is that creation is very good, and God intended it to be our home and our *only* home. "The world" is not creation, but the sphere of the powers and principalities. All monasticism rests on a mistaken confusion of creation with this world, and so they suppose by withdrawing in some symbolic fashion from creation that they are leaving the world. But creation is precisely not the world but its antithesis, and so what they do is essentially the opposite of salvation. They withdraw from creation into the desert taking "this world" with them, and there they dwell apart from creation, but in a newly erected kingdom of the prince of this world. Isn't it evident to you that everything you were saying about the bureaucracy and dehumanization of the monastic institution is precisely the very essence of "this world," the purest expression of the powers and the principalities? You have not withdrawn from this world into heaven, you have withdrawn from creation into hell! No wonder the young monks left — they left, not because they lost their vocations, but hopefully because they found them and knew that they would not be expressed in that corner of "this world" which calls itself "monastery."

Having delivered myself of this blast, let me say that I don't think that man has lost all need for solitude and contemplation. In fact those who believe that the work of Christ is hand to hand combat with the powers and the principalities in the arena of real historical action in order to make God's good creation again and again appear on earth, these people are in sore need for the inner strength and discipline that solitude and contemplation can give. But it must be evident that this will be as an auxiliary help and place of temporary withdrawal for inner deepening which is not an end in itself but directed back towards the real action. Hence, a monasticism which would serve the church in this way must admit that it is not the central arena of salvation but serves the main action as auxiliary stations, like Academia, as a place of learning which is not an end in itself but a ministry for the sake of a larger community. In order for it to do this ministry well, Academia must be free. It cannot be narrowly pragmatic and utilitarian. It must, within in its own sphere, even have a learning and a thought which is its own *raison d'être*, but even this freedom and non-utilitarianism is only in the larger context of being a ministry. If monasticism could view itself as a ministry, as a place to which the whole church could have recourse as a place of contemplation, but contemplation for the sake of the main arena of salvation which takes place precisely in the sphere of historical action, then it could take on a new relevance for modern man. As long as it remains rooted in its original understanding of being itself the most authentic arena of this event, it is, and I believe must necessarily be, unacceptable to modern man, not as a pagan man but precisely as a Christian man and a radically Christian man.

Best,
Rosemary Ruether

P.S. I enclose an article on ministry and community — it will be in a festschrift on ministry that Herder and Herder is putting out in honor of Father Reinhold.[13] I think you can see the same conflict of charisma and institution that you were wrestling with in your monastic renewal, and rightly so, for it is precisely the same thing, which is to say, being the church is being for the kingdom of God in the midst of and in struggle with (not withdrawal from) the objectifying forces that represent the prince of the world.

Could you return the carbon when you have read it?

Dear Rosemary:

*Y*our long letter on the monastic renewal piece reached me today. I am just out of the hospital and can't type yet. I

13. Rosemary Ruether, "Ministry in the Church of the Future," in Gerald Sloyan, ed., *Secular Priest in the New Church* (New York: Herder and Herder, 1967), 232–49.

intend to write you a decent answer to this and to the other letter, as soon as I comfortably can. I'll spare you my handwriting.

Glad you set forth the toughest arguments against monasticism, as they are the ones that have to be faced today. However, in your absolutist version I don't recognize monasticism in a form that any monk in his right mind today would accept. Historically that view has existed however. Is it the original one? I rather doubt it. Anyway, I agree perfectly on your "Academia" solution which is what I am working for in practice myself. As to the monastic *institution* — you don't disagree I'm trying to save that do you? There is a charism of freedom which is what interests me, and that is what you seem to be burying on arbitrary grounds — I smile, a little of the Principalities and Powers there, I think. Or at least I feel they might be there. The great question is freedom from the domination of that hubris by which the Principalities and Powers enslave fallen man individually and collectively. On that we agree. Let us also admit frankly that foggy and ambiguous ideas of the "world" can certainly promote that enslavement. There's the area for theological clarity now.

Lots of love,
Tom

ॐ

c. March 4, 1967

Dear Thomas Merton:

I couldn't read all of your letter, but a certain state of shock came through to me from it. I hope that what seems a polemic will be seen through by you, and you will, in an unthreatened way, see the systematic exposition that lies behind it, a position which coheres with everything else I have written and which presumably you have liked.

– 31 –

The radical way in which I presented the monastic position is, I believe, the systematic presentation of the logic of asceticism. It has seldom been actualized for the reason that, fully actualized, it would lead to the dissolution of the world, and that fact is really the revelation of its systematic aim, namely salvation *from* the world which expresses itself fundamentally in a dissolution of creation. Only Albigensians and similar groups have tried to live out this logic to the fullest and even they had to make a distinction between the full members of the church and the half-way men who were allowed to produce the next generation. But, because monasticism has remained rooted in this point of view, while, at the same time, being a part of a church which has, in effect, become a part of the world, i.e., the religion of a society, it has existed in a state of ambiguity, and now that it is indeed regarded by no one as the highest Christian state, even monks themselves being reluctant to apply that original logic, it has indeed lost its soul, i.e., its original self-understanding, and yet cannot free itself from this logic in a radical enough way to find a new fully systematic way of integrating itself into the church. Basically the problem of monasticism is the same as the problem of the church *vis à vis* the world, and this is only to be expected since monasticism arose as a new way of expressing eschatological alienation after the church as a whole had become a *religio licita* and so failed to be able to express this principle as a society. The principle of eschatological alienation is itself the principle that must be radically rethought by us in order to rediscover both the meaning of the church and the meaning and role for monasticism within the new church. Basically this is a reintegration of eschatological happening into a perspective of history. The eschatological is not the dissolution of history but the center of renewal of history. Thus the church stands as the eschatological community over against the world not to decrease the world but to recreate it. Within this context of the prophetic community the monastic community then could play a vital function as being a place of reflection for the whole church which then sends us back into the work of renewal. It would then be not a total vocation in itself but a vital part of the total rhythm, but just as there are some full time academics who serve the many disciples that come and go, so there would be full time "masters of reflection" who would serve the whole community who could have recourse to the monastic community as a place of examination.

What I said about the demonizing of the monastic community you should have recognized as an application of the same demonizing that I spoke of *vis à vis* the institutional church in the Vahanian article.[14] The solution, as I indicate in the "community and ministry" article, is not de-institutionalization or "spiritual community" (an unhistorical possibility) but a theology which puts the institution in its proper perspective.

Sincerely,
Rosemary Ruether

❧❧

March 9, 1967

Dear Rosemary:

*T*hanks for the new letter, received this morning. I can type now, for a while, and will try to get enough down on paper to serve as a reply that will forward the discussion.

Shock? No, not that. But just a sort of dismay because I felt that your last letter — perhaps written hastily — was not in tune with what you had been saying, and after reading the article on "Community and Ministry" (which I liked very much), I felt that the letter was not in tune with this either. The impression I got from the letter, the one with "Community and Ministry," which you thought shocked me, was that you were putting monks

---

14. Rosemary Ruether, "Vahanian: The Worldly Church and the Churchly World," *Continuum* 4, no. 1 (Spring 1966): 50–62. Subsequently reprinted as chapter 11 of Ruether's *The Church against Itself.*

on an entirely different basis from the rest of the Church, and saying that our charism-vs-institution struggle was radically different from anybody else's, because the basis on which we stood was theologically impossible and, in fact, heretical, pagan, diabolical. Next thing, I thought, I'll be burnt at the stake by radical Christians. Once you admit that we are all pretty much in the same pickle, and that we face varying forms of the same struggle, I breathe easier. In a word, what we all need is the simple elementary "freedom to begin where we are" and to really rethink in a radical and creative way our place in the Church — and adapt institutional structures, as far as possible, to serve this creative understanding.

But honestly, your view of monasticism is, to me, so abstract and so, in a way, arbitrary (though plenty of basis in texts can be found) that it is simply poles apart from the existential, concrete, human dimension which the problem has for us here. The thing that dismays me is the problem of groping around for a place to start talking about it all. Perhaps the best thing would be to start from my own personal motives. Let me put it this way: I am so far from being "an ascetic" that I am in many ways an anti-ascetic humanist, and one of the things in monasticism that has always meant most to me is that monastic life is in closer contact with God's good creation and is in many ways simpler, saner, and more human than life in the supposedly comfortable, pleasurable world. One of the things I love about my life, and, therefore, one of the reasons why I would not change it for anything, is the fact that I live in the woods and according to a tempo of sun and moon and season in which it is naturally easy and possible to walk in God's light, so to speak, in and through his creation. That is why the narcissist bit in prayer and contemplation is no problem out here, because, in fact, I seldom have to fuss with any such thing as "recollecting myself" and all that rot. All you do is breathe and look around and wash dishes, type, etc. Or just listen to the birds. I say this in all frankness, realizing that I can be condemned for having it so much better than almost anybody. That is what I feel guilty about, I suppose, but certainly not that I have repudiated God's good creation. Sure, it is there in the cities too, but in such a strained, unnatural, tense shape. I won't go into that angle of it. But, in point of fact, when I buy your "academic" argument for monasticism it is partly because I want to share this lovely life with all my friends, and I would be willing to have monks run national parks or something if it would help us do so. Absolutely the last thing in my own mind is the idea that the monk de-creates all that God has made. On the contrary, monks are, and I am, in my own mind, the remnant of desperate conservationists. You ought to know what hundreds of pine saplings I have planted, myself and with the novices, only to see them bulldozed by some ass a year later. In a word, to my mind the monk is one of those who not only saves the world in the theological sense, but saves it literally, protecting it against the destructiveness of the rampaging city of greed, war, etc. And this loving care for natural creatures becomes, in some sense, a warrant of his theological mission and ministry as a man of contemplation. I refuse in practice to accept any theory or method of contemplation that simply divides soul against body, interior against exterior, and then tries to transcend itself by pushing creatures out into the dark. What dark? As soon as the split is made the dark is abysmal in everything, and the only way to get back into the light is to be once again a normal human being who likes to smell the flowers and look at girls, if they are around, and who likes the clouds, etc. On the other hand, the real purpose of asceticism is not cutting off one's relation to created things and other people, but normalizing and healing it. The contemplative life, in my way of thinking (with Greek Fathers, etc.), is simply the restoration of man, in Christ, to the state in which he was originally intended to live. Of course this presents problems, but I am in the line of the paradise tradition in monastic thought, which is also part and parcel of the desert tradition and is also eschatological, because the monk here and now is supposed to be living the life of the new creation in which the right relation to all the rest of God's creatures is fully restored. Hence, desert father stories about tame lions and all that jazz.

You will say this is not theology. Well, let's look a little at the literature. Though it is easier to find statements that seem to be and, in fact, are radically negative about material creation, I would say one must not oversimplify. This business of saying, as you do, that the monk is in the same boat with the Manichean but just refuses, out of a Christian instinct and good sense, to be logical about it, is, I think, wrong. About early monastic literature, two things have to be observed first of all:

1. There are several different traditional blocs of texts. The Syrian tend to be very negative, gnostic, Manichean (exception made for Ephrem who is utterly different). But note, for instance, the development in the ideas of Chrysostom, for example. Then there is the reaction of Basil and the Cappadocians (blending Syrian with Egyptian-Greek lines). The Greek-Egyptian hermit school. Origenist and Evagrian, less negative than the Syrians, more balanced. Here in the *Life of Anthony,* a classic source if there ever was one, Athanasius goes to great pains to have Anthony say that all creation is very good, and nothing is to be rejected, even the devils are good in so far as they are creatures, etc., etc. The Coptic school, especially in the Pachomian text, the most biblical of the bunch, quite Old Testament, in fact, and with an Old Testament respect for creation and God's blessing upon the creatures.

2. In the literature itself there are questions of literary form and other such matters that are very important. Stories are told and statements are made that push one idea to an extreme. The balance is restored in other stories that push the opposite idea to its extreme. Thus there are stories that prove that no one can possibly be saved unless he is a monk, and other stories in which the greatest monastic saints are told in vision to go down town and visit some unlikely-looking layperson (married and all) who turns out to be a greater saint than he by just living an ordinary life. A restudy and rethinking of these sources will, I am sure,

show that you are much too sweeping when you say that monasticism is simply a repudiation of the world in the sense of God's good creation. On the contrary, it is a repudiation — more often — of the world in the sense of a decadent, imperial society in which the Church has become acclimatized to an atmosphere that is basically idolatrous. Now, all right, the history of monasticism does show that the monks themselves got "demonized" by being incorporated into the power structure and all that. This I have said myself, and I agree with you. But also the reactions are much more important than you seem to realize. For instance, the very significant lay-hermit movement in the eleventh century, lay solitaries who were also itinerant preachers to the poor and the outcasts who had no one to preach to them (since there was no preaching in the parishes and even in many cathedrals). These were forerunners not only of Franciscanism but also of Protestantism and pre-Protestant sects like the Waldensians, etc. You have probably run into some of this, but not connected it with the hermits.

Once this more existential view of the whole monastic situation becomes possible, then I think it is possible to agree with you that monasticism has "lost its soul" in so far as it has become committed to an iron-bound institutionalism built on a perverse doctrine of authority-humility-obedience. The bind here is worse than anywhere else in the Church, insofar as the emphasis on perfect obedience as "the" monastic virtue (which of course it is not) puts the monk bound hand and foot in the power of his "prelate" (now no longer charismatic and chosen spiritual father but his boss and feudal lord and maybe general in chief). Then when renunciation of the world is fitted into this context by being a prohibition of any sight or sound of anything outside the monastic walls, any concern with any human activity outside the walls, and so on, plus a Jansenistic repudiation of all pleasure, then you do get a real monastic hell: I don't deny that at all, I have lived in one. But again, the answer is to start with saving the poor blighters that are caught in such a mess and to save the beautiful life that has been turned into a hell for them when it should be what it was first intended to be.

The terms in which I have been stating this have been deliberately "humanistic" in order to emphasize the fact that we are NOT simply refusing to have anything to do with God's good creation, and that the idea of "salvation from the world instead of salvation of the world" makes a nice slogan, but it does not really apply at all to our case properly understood, only to the distortion. I agree of course that the distortion has been terribly widespread, and is.

From here on out, we can get at the really important idea of eschatological alienation. Another time. And also a further development of the idea of the relation of the monk to the rest of the Church.

In passing, I admit that I myself see a serious problem in the idea of a monastic Church constituted outside of, and over against, a Church in the world. We'll have to go into that too.

More in tune with this letter: an example of what I myself am doing in my "secularized" existence as a hermit. I am not only leading a more "worldly" life (me and the rabbits), but am subtly infecting the monastery with worldly ideas. I still am requested to give one talk a week in community, and have covered things like Marxism and the idea of dialogue *à la* Garaudy, Hromadka, and so on, and especially all kinds of literary material, Rilke for some time and, now for a long time, a series of lectures on Faulkner and his theological import. This is precisely what I think a hermit ought to do for the community which has seen fit deliberately and consciously to afford him liberty. I have a liberty which can fruitfully serve my brothers, and by extension I think it indicates what might be the monk's role for the rest of the Church. Not only literature, of course, all sorts of things. I think too that being in a position to grab on to some Zen I have an obligation to do this, though Zen is not something one has. It is more a way of being (it is least of all a religious doctrine or ideology). More about that some other time.

Sorry this was so long, but I hope I have been able to make clear that the only world I am trying to get saved from is that of the principalities and powers, who may or may not have computers and jet planes at their disposal, that too is another question. The rest of it, I am with you in wanting to save and in wanting to have the freedom to work for effectively.

I am returning the manuscript of your article, which is very good indeed. I agree perfectly.

With all my best wishes, and without shock,

Yours,
Tom

❧

Mid-March, 1967

Dear Thomas Merton:

*T*hank you for your long letter and also for the manuscript so promptly returned. I have a tendency to send off my last carbon and then need it when I want to write something else. I am going to do some final rewriting on the book manuscript, which unfortunately is still moving slowly due to the excitement of the Sheed and Ward, London people in local ecclesiastical affairs. Publishing and revolution may make a good combination for them, but not for the person who is trying to get something done through them.

As to your last remarks, basically I also take the paradise tradition, the restoration of creation as my understanding of redemption and far from thinking that talk of tame lions is not good theology, I think it is the very best theology! However, that monasticism got mixed up with anti-matter theology and hence got involved in a fearful ambiguity towards creation is something that we don't have to dispute about. It is quite obvious to us both, and so the re-creating the world position (the authentic function of the eschatological community) has generally been smothered. It is the logic of the gnostic position (which monasticism got confused with eschatological alienation) that leads to de-creation, and I think if you read your same sources with these lenses on instead of the rosy lenses of the paradise tradition, you will see this position equally represented and tending to cancel out the other — this is quite obvious to me, for example, in my studies of the Cappadocians, and it takes the form particularly in a hostility towards the *politike arete* [political virtue] of ancient culture which I consider to be disastrous — a tendency which you also exhibit.

What we have to reject, obviously, is "this world" qua principalities and powers, and not God's good creation — but principalities and powers are not to be equated with historical activity and civilization. It is the arena of historical action which is the real arena of redemption. In the Psalms and Prophets, the central expression of the coming of God's Kingdom is to be found in the historical arena, in the nations laying down their arms and the vindication of the oppressed. The nature passages about lions laying down with lambs are only meaningful in this broader context of historical redemption in which the real threats that deprive the world of its humanity are overcome. This understanding of the reconciliation of the hostile forces of the world has little in common with a nature idyll. The equation of "creation" with sub-human nature and the rejection of historical responsibility, I consider one of the dangerous tendencies of monasticism in its original form, and one which has little to do with a biblical understanding of eschatological hope. It seems to me that a paradise tradition that is mixed up with agrarian romanticism fails to take the principalities and powers seriously enough. If we are to overcome them, we have to stay hooked into where they are. Paradise is brought out of the wilderness, not in a symbolic sense of planting trees in wildernesses, but in the real sense of struggling against the dehumanizing forces in the city of man. Just as you say that you don't want to run away from the monastic principalities and powers, but try to stay with the poor blighters to help save them, then surely a more important application of the same principle is that we have to stay hooked into and love the world of technology (which is not itself bad but very good — as all advances of civilization are good as part of God's historical creativity), in order to overcome their demonizing tendencies and win them for the humanization of the world. Thus, although I think that the same principle applies both to your struggle with punctilious abbots and mine with the forces of the city, I fear that these principalities and powers of the ecclesiastical organization are too insignificant, and that a church involvement that oscillates between bunny rabbits and abbots has to do with small-time demons and sub-human paradises, while the real demons and the significant arena of redemption goes ignored. We turn away from the big-time demons and allow them to reign undisturbed, while we are occupied with our birds and bees and petty ecclesiastical housekeeping. I don't know if we really can allow ourselves to be absorbed in these kinds of demons and paradises, while the big-time demons and the central arena where redemption needs to be wrested from the wilderness goes by the boards, and we gather in our country seats while the work of civilization collapses — which was precisely the objection of the Roman civic leaders to monasticism in the 4th century, and I think an absolutely valid objection. In short, I think a theology of opposition to the principalities and powers and a bringing of paradise out of the wilderness is a theology on which we can both adhere, but I think we do disagree as to what this means — first of all, the principalities and powers are not somebody or something else but we ourselves; it is we ourselves, that we must struggle against, and secondly, we do not bring paradise out of the wilderness by taking off to the hills, but by struggling with the principalities and powers where they really are, and it is only in this way that paradise is brought out of the wilderness, the real and not the figurative wilderness.

Best,
Rosemary

🝀

Dear Rosemary:

*T*hanks for your letter which came the other day during the visit of an old friend of mine, a tough minded, irreligious Karnap trained journalist [Seymour (Sy) Freedgood]. He and I went into the monastic question very thoroughly, including the *politike arete* bit and all the rest. Because he knows me, and knew me when I was a communist (of sorts) and all that, he knows very well that I am not "hostile to *politike arete*." But he saw, as I do, the real trouble: my lack of ability to communicate what I mean and to say what really needs to be said because I am out of touch, in other words it is not at all a question of repudiating political life but of participating in a way that makes sense here. And I would add, what is coming through to me now in your letters is that we both seem to be accepting a naive and unreal separation between "city" and "country" that no longer means anything in the modern world. It seems to me in your last letter you were just using the old dualism, turned inside out. As if I were living in a sixth century virgin forest with wolves. This is not "sub-human nature" out here, it is farm country, and farmers are people with the same crucial twentieth century problems as everybody else. Also, tree planting and reforestation are not simply sentimental gestures in a region that has been ravaged by the coal and lumber companies. If reforestation were merely symbolic, I doubt if it would have the importance it seems to have, for instance, in Mao's China.

And while we are on that, another thing. I wonder if you realize that you (at least from your letters) are a very academic, cerebral, abstract type. You talk about God's good creation, the goodness of the body, and all that, but I wonder if you have any realization at all of the fact that by working on the land a person is deeply and sensually involved with matter. I return to the point I made in my last letter and which you dismissed as romanticism. It is not romanticism at all, my friend. Of course I insist that in my unawareness of how revolutionary the actual situation may be, I am prescribing something — a luxury maybe — for which there just is *not* time. It is something you city people need and need very badly indeed. And for all their gnosticism, monks (at least in the West where manual work has been held in honor) have had this sensual contact with matter and have not in fact despised matter at all except in theory (and except where they have been warped by their own theory). Hence, I would say that in my life the cultivation and expansion of the senses, and sensual awareness of things and people, and sensual response, are probably a whole lot more important than they are in yours. That is why I don't take very seriously your academic dismissal of my statements on the grounds of something some fool monk said in the fifth century when, in any case, everyone was saying the same things because their senses were so strong and their passions so powerful that one could be afraid of them. It is easier today to talk about the body and all that when one is insulated by technology from the direct impact of nature.

To return to the city-country dichotomy. In actual fact, is there anything you can do in the city, more effectively than I can do in the country, to stop the war in Vietnam? Except perhaps march with a sign in front of the White House (which is something I too ought to be allowed to do). But in reality are we not reduced to pretty much the same gestures, with pretty much the same hope of achieving anything? My negative ideas about political life today are trying precisely to say that political action is too often rendered futile by the massive corruption and dishonesty and fakery which neutralize it everywhere. But I do not mean by that to say that political action is ineffective and hopeless: just that something else is needed. Same with technology: it is not evil, but it is not beyond all criticism either. If used cynically and opportunistically for power and wealth, it becomes a disastrous weapon *against* humanity and is the instrument by which the demons crush and humiliate and destroy humanity. Witness the Vietnam war. Obviously, it has to be made clear that the old negative Jansenistic pietism that just turns away from the machine and murmurs prayers to the Blessed Mother or St. Joseph the Worker or something has to be shown up for what it is. But the problem of getting technology back into the power of man so that it may be used for man's own good is by all odds the great problem of the day. And one of the things that is demanded is a real iconoclastic attack on the ambiguities and confusion surrounding the misuse of technology. I am aware of the fact that since I don't know enough about it, I make attempts at doing this which are merely futile, and then I try to cover my frustration by louder cries and more vehemence which just makes it worse.

But basically, I think it should be the job of the monk to do this kind of iconoclastic criticism. It has to be seen, not in some stupid pietistic way, but as people like Mumford see it.

You will be interested to hear that Vahanian stopped here the other day. He was on his way to the airport, and we did not have much time, a couple of hours, early in the morning when he was still half asleep. I enjoyed meeting him, and we talked mostly about Faulkner on whom I am working now.

Going back to your letter, let me repeat once again:

1. It is not a matter of rejecting historical responsibility and of equating the activity of the principalities and powers with history itself. But it is in history precisely that we confront their action, because history is the struggle of the old and the new, the fallen and the redeemed, the principalities and powers against man snatched out of their hands by Christ and in Him. Hence

the problem is not just one of false spirituality versus incarnation, but much more dangerously, of a false and demonic parody of creation and incarnation and redemption, a demonic parody of the Kingdom: and this is where a naive optimism about technology is a source of great problems. True historical responsibility cannot coexist with blindness on this crucial point.

2. Certainly the demons down here are small time. But it is by confronting them that a monk has to open the way to his own kind of involvement in the big time struggle, or, as Vahanian said the other day, to be effectively iconoclastic in the modern world. I am personally keenly aware that if I merely threw in the sponge down here and went out to engage in something ostensibly more effective, it would be a real betrayal, not of abstract obligations, but of the Kingdom in which the monastic life, however marginal, retains its importance. In many ways I would prefer to simplify the question, take matters into my own hands, and get going. On the other hand, I observe so many people in the monastic Order doing this and ending up in the most ridiculous futilities — far worse than the ones against which they are protesting. Maybe there is a *kairos* coming, but I have no notion where or when; I am in the most uncomfortable and unenviable position of waiting without any justification, without a convincing explanation, and without any assurance except that it seems to be what God wants of me and that this kind of desperation is what it means for me to be without idols — I hope. I don't expect anyone on earth to congratulate me for this, and as far as I am concerned, it is just damned stupid, but it seems to be what I have to do. But I do think, given a more favorable situation, the monastic life can play a very helpful part in the worldly struggle precisely because of the different perspective which it has and should preserve. What is needed is for the doors to open and for people to get around more and learn a little.

All the best,
Tom

P.S. I am sorry to add more, but I am doing it in the fear that you may have thought the earlier pages a little insolent. They were not intended to be so. I do dimly realize — if only from scattered reading — that the situation now must be one in which my own small concerns with monasticism may seem completely irrelevant. And I am not defending them. Because they are not just monastic concerns, they are human and universal. What makes it difficult to express this is the fact that, for instance, "being a hermit" seems to mean trying to be a very peculiar and special kind of artificial man, whereas for me what it means is being nothing but man, or nothing but a mere man reduced to his simple condition as man, that is to say as a nonmonk even, a non-layman, a non-categorized man, a plain simple man: not as an ideal status or a condition of "striving for spiritual perfection," but a reduction to the bare condition of man as a starting point where everything has to begin: incomplete and insufficient in the sense of being outside social cadres. But then, entering into these in a free and tentative way, in an exploratory way, to establish new and simple relationships. As of one who is not a doctor, a banker, a politician, or this or that, but a "mere man." And this condition of mere humanity does not require solitude in the country, it can be and should be realized anywhere. This is just my way of doing it. What would seem to others to be the final step into total alienation seems to me to be the beginning of the resolution of all alienation and the preparation for a real return, without masks and without defenses, into the world as mere man. Pardon the mystique, but I got this idea and thought I would share it. Your critical mind will chop it down to size, but I think there is something valid there.

Dear Thomas:

I am really kind of disappointed in you. Do you realize how defensive you are, how you are forever proving, proving how good your life is, etc.? You really won't hear the kind of balance that I am trying to establish in my letters, but immediately distort it into your own caricature, so that you can again have the riposte. I'm not interested in any of that. I am trying to work out a perspective whereby the traditional dichotomies can be seen as dynamic and existential and will not be forever translated into ontological or substantive kinds of dualisms which seem to me the source of false clashes of body and spirit, grace and law, etc. But when I try to show this inner relation of grace and demons, you refuse to get the point and seize upon some glimmering of "false optimism of technology" which is at no point what I said, and then proceed to read back to me essentially the very point of view I was trying to expound as though that were a refutation, when in fact it is exactly what I was saying if you could have listened to it without being so bloody defensive and on edge. O.K. great. Let's all recreate the world together, but if you can come down off your high horse a minute and listen to me, it should be simple common sense that the city is the important place to be hooked into for recreating the world, because it is where the center of power is and, thus, where the center of "powers" is to be encountered and grappled with. This doesn't mean that the country isn't also a part of the world! It does mean that it is somewhat less in touch and, particularly, where the country (and perhaps this is more acute in suburbia) operates as a nostalgic turning away from the problems of our time to a never, never land of a simpler life of the past. Again I am not attacking you. I am talking about a phenomenon of our times. People flee to the country in our society, so they can exist in a false simplicity and security, so they can keep an illusion of simple town life and pretend that the technological age has never come, like

Marie Antoinette in her shepherd's cottage. To live in the inner city, in the midst of the technological wasteland, therefore, is a kind of witnessing, not that we are doing so much more about it, but at least it represents a determination to stick with the real situation. It is true that you can also be very related to all these things, while living on the highest mountain through reading, news media, etc., but in some very vital way, we are what we see, and things come home to you when you see them, in a way that they don't when you never encounter them firsthand. Don't get excited. It is just a small fact. Nobody is undercutting your existence. As for *politike arete* I was speaking as a church historian. I see that as a fundamental tension, and I find it very significant in the drama of the ancient world, that, at the last lap, monasticism and the old aristocracy faced each other in this particular way. I also find it interesting that the monastic a-cultural point of view was all but superseded by a Roman view of civic responsibility which was taken over and made so much the church's own that monasticism, far from being equated with irresponsibility for culture, became the preserver of it. Witness the interesting relation between a Jerome and an Ambrose. I would like to discuss all these things with you, because I find them interesting. But you seem too threatened at the moment to discuss them objectively.

I again get the strong impression from your letter that you are in some period of crisis whose implications you are fighting off with long arguments. I really have only a glimmering of what it is, so I feel very diffident about what to suggest. First, let me say that the crisis I sense is not primarily to do with monasticism as an answer in general, but with *you*, with the rhythm of your personal development. You seem to me to have reached a crisis point in that development where you need a new point of view. This is a crisis, because if it is not met adequately, it will surely mean a regression to a less full existence for you, while if its meaning is properly discerned, it will be a new *kairos* leading to a new level of perception. It seems to me that part of this will entail getting into another place, so that part of the time you would be related to a different kind of society; this is not a question of leaving hermeticism permanently, but just some new contacts perhaps to be reintegrated back into your vocation on a new level. I think your subconscious is sensing the need for a change, and your superconscious is fighting it off (those as crudities, but they will symbolize the dichotomies that I mean), and this is why you manifest a great deal of defensiveness toward monasticism particularly when the discussion veers on something that touches your present "rightness." I hope this is helpful. There is not much more I can say about this, because you will have to fill in the blanks for yourself. Nobody can really discover what is needed for you, but you yourself, although we can strike up against each other in the manner I suggested in a letter some time ago. The Word of God that comes through our words for each other has to be somehow decoded by the Holy Spirit as a gift beyond the present merit of speaker or hearer.

Best,
Rosemary

P.S. Enclosed are a few materials you may find interesting. The litany I used recently at a chapel service at Howard (as a member of the seminary faculty, I am expected to fulfil a few such "clerical" functions). The image making and breaking was my sermon on this occasion. Sorry you find me so abstract. If I weren't a woman would it have occurred to you to accuse me of being cerebral? Interesting resentment there.... The Emmaus House is a great place, which has recently asked me to be on its board. They are inner-city "monks." I wouldn't mention the resentment bit if it wasn't so absolutely predictable. I am just as fleshy as you, baby, and I am also just as much a "thinking animal" as you.

Dear Rosemary:

I am really very grateful for your last letter, the one that came in with the litanies today. And I am sorry for being such a creep, but it is true that you did make me feel very defensive. First of all, I guess I have not caught on to your approach "the traditional dichotomies . . . dynamic and existential." Don't give up: I'll try again and promise not to prove anymore that living in the woods is not really abandoning the Church (which is probably what I really want to do I guess. Maybe that is why I make such a fuss about justifying my position. I think you've helped me to cool off on that one).

Of course, I agree with you perfectly: obviously, the city is the place where things are really happening, and, obviously too, a certain distance and marginality is good for monasticism because the country is *not* city and the perspective is slightly different. I agree with you too about nostalgia, pastoral simplicity, and all that. So don't give up on me, I will be objective.

What helped most somehow was the tone of the letter. Before, you were simply professional or something, and I am not a pro at anything except writing: I am no theologian, and, lately, I haven't even been reading about monasticism, or monastic literature at all. I suppose I will get around to that again one of these days, with new perspectives. Right now I am working on Faulkner and also writing on Camus and am, I suppose, again sneaking out the back door of the Church without telling myself that this is what I am doing. I don't feel guilty about this though and am conscious of it. Anyway, in this last letter you were talking more my own language (about being so bloody defensive, etc.), and I feel perfectly at home with it. Thanks also for the last sentence of the P.S.: "I am as fleshy as you, baby. . . . " OK, I recognize an idiom I am accustomed to and am not scared anymore. I promise I won't get up in the air again. I don't know why you frighten me so. ("Cerebral" probably because I

– 50 –

resented my mother's intellectuality, or what I later interpreted as that.)

You are perhaps more right than I think about the "crisis," though I have the impression I am not in much more of a crisis than I have been for the last ten years or more. It is perfectly true that I need to get out of here and get around a bit, and I know it only too well. This is one of the most frustrating things about the complete irrationality of my Abbot who will not and cannot even discuss such a thing with equanimity. Since I can't even communicate with him on the point and discuss it reasonably, and can't get anything out of higher superiors either, it is a bit frustrating.

Thanks again. Come on with St. Jerome and Ambrose: I'd be glad to go into all that with you.

Joy in the Lord and all my very best,
Tom

P.S. I haven't read your enclosures yet. Will report later.

❦

March 25, 1967

Dear Rosemary:

*Y*es, I realize that you are right about the crisis bit, because I am in one of those situations when so much is surfacing that I can't even read, and I have to talk to someone. Since you have been the catalyst, I trust your patience. You will have to be my confessor for awhile: will you please? I think you have already implicitly taken on the job anyway.

Back to your letters and my insults. My misinterpretation worked like this. First: I recognized in you someone I could really, I thought, talk to at last. Second: I felt that you were putting me, as monk, in a category of people to whom you refused to talk. Image: she is saying she won't recognize me as a human being until I leave the monastery. Problem: unrecognized assumption of my own that I have to get out of here. Below that: recognition that life here is to some extent (not entirely) a lie and that I can no longer just say the community lies and I don't. With that: sense of being totally unable to do anything about it that is not a feeble gesture. But also a genuine realization that this *is* my vocation, but that I have not yet found the way of being really true to it. Rock bottom: I don't know what is down there. I just don't know.

Yes, the monastic life here is an idol.

Provisional solution: the people are not idols, they are real, they are my brothers, though they are also, for the most part, idiots (my Karnap friend told me last week, without any opposition from me, "you live among idiots"). Solidarity for me begins here. Author's vanity: would like to be part of a real groovy worldly in-group and can't. Being out here is really in some way exile, humiliation, desperation. Yet also, I love the place on another level, which I defended vociferously before. I do need contact with you all outside. All I have is a kind of blind faith that this will work out somehow. Political machinations and pressures are not something I am good at, so I don't see a way to break out and don't know how. Incidentally, one reason why the Abbot so easily consented in letting me be a hermit is that this gives him extra leverage. "Hermits *never* travel." (Which is pure crap; hermits are the most travelling of all Christians.)

All this outcry about freedom.

Refusal to grapple with the idea of monastic renewal because I see that too much is really involved and that what is going on here now is superficial; what is really in question is the survival of the kind of thing we have here. They are trying to save it, or at least the general structure. I realize obscurely that it can't be saved, has to be entirely rebuilt from the bottom up. Yes, I know Emmaus House: I even think I am on the Board of Advisors myself, but God alone knows.

Your sermon on images is just beautiful. Page 4 is very much like what I mean by Zen, and your accounting for hellenistic theology in the fathers is most apt and helpful. "Imageless void of the Spirit" is Zen, except that Zen is more radical, like it sounds as if there were a Spirit that had a void, though you mean the Spirit is the Void. Expressed in happenings for which there is no museum possible. When they have happened they're gone (where?) No treasury in other words. No religious possessions. Page 6 is real monastic theology: and we just now are in the middle of elaborately rebuilding our temple in the desert, only "modern."

OK, now I get you. I understand. You won't have trouble with me on this point, so fire away with whatever you want to tell me about Jerome, Ambrose, all those cats. I wrote on them in my new book which I'll send when it is out.[15]

I think this should clear things up a bit. I am not mad at you for being an "intellectual woman," but only for seeming to reject me. I don't take sweetly to rejection, I tell you. I need and value your friendship, and I will also, on my part, be more or less grown up about it and try to give you what I can in my turn, once I know what you want. And now I think I do. (Before, I got the impression you didn't want anything from me except that I shut up and admit you were right about something or other).

All the best, joy in the Lord, yours,
Tom

P.S. You may conceivably get an offer of the chair of Catholic Theology at Vanderbilt Divinity School. Someone from there was here, and I recommended you. Only they haven't got the money for it yet.

※※

---

15. Thomas Merton, *The Climate of Monastic Prayer* (Spencer, Mass.: Cistercian Publications, 1969). Also published as *Contemplative Prayer* (Herder and Herder, 1969).

Early April 1967

Dear Thomas:

I really appreciate your gesture towards St. Steve's. Did I ever send you our Good Friday, Easter celebrations sheet? I enclose one that turned up. It was put on by St. Stephen's and the People together. The People are going to do the music at St. Stephen's and set up a People school there. A People school is a school which will train groups in music, arts and liturgy to set up and lead events like this. A sort of school to train people in the arts of "making happenings" (that is a sort of works-grace problem, but in so far as happenings can be made, we will teach people how to make them).

I have taken your advice on publishers. [Philip] Scharper from Sheed and Ward wrote me asking if I wanted to do a book that would bring together all phases of the current sex problem, and I wrote back saying "I do not now nor at any time in the foreseeable future wish to write any books on marriage, divorce, birth control, women, celibacy, abortion, or sex." I think Father Cavanaugh, in the recent issue of *Look,* has covered the field of Catholic sexology sufficiently — what a depressing article! It really made you feel that the church was so hopelessly neurotic and was screwing up so many people's lives that the world would really be better off if it disappeared from the face of the earth.

I think some conversation would be good on the monastic-eschatological bit. I am inclined to see the whole thing as one of mankind's magnificent illusions, but the key illusion which generates enormous power to make great creative leaps in history — but unfortunately leaps in all sorts of directions, many of them ending with the last state of that man worse than the first. People who are kingdom-struck can do things which men guided by a rational estimate of the possible could never achieve... and sometimes, as you said, they leave behind some nice furniture when it is all over. But sometimes worse things are left behind. As Loisy put it: "The irony of Christianity is that

– 54 –

Jesus preached the kingdom and the (Roman) church was the result."

What do you think of the hippies? speaking of eschat types? In many ways it is an adamic movement, like the brethren of the free spirit in the middle ages, people who live with no possessions, sharing everything, a kind of primeval innocence, love is the key note, a love which feels itself to have surpassed all capacity for sinfulness. The LSD thing hooks up with the mystical tradition, and these people consciously draw on the monastic traditions both Christian and Buddhist, the chants, the language of contemplation, much more than the previous movement of alienation, of the fifties, — the beats. Hippies are mystical and "full of grace" in a way quite different from the beats. It is fascinating that at the moment when the churches are all in a great surge of activism as the modality of "relevance" the left fringe of our society suddenly wants to sit cross-legged in a world of votive lights and soar up to God within their souls.

Better stay in the woods —

Love,
Rosemary

☙❧

Early April 1967

Dear Thomas:

*M*uch relieved at your last two letters. We are sort of up another ridge. I am also glad you like the image article. I have reworked it in extended form as the new ending for the book,[16] also threw out the Barth chapter and put in a revised and enlarged working of the *Ecumenist* article ... did you see that

---

16. Rosemary Ruether, *The Church against Itself*, Chapter 12.

one?[17] Apropos of the topic I treated there, it is really hard to decide, in a way, the relation between commitment to institution, even when dead and deadly, and the right to seek charismatic community. I think that is a problem in which we are all involved. I battled this out for a long time, and so many Catholics really exist in a split situation, existing as "hermit," i.e., outcast on the fringes of an institution, participating vicariously in some other charismatic community, not yet willing to forsake the one and integrate concrete community life into some other situation where these things could be gotten together, because there is still a real feeling of affection, commitment, identity, concern for the structure where you are, yet one has no future there, no hope of being able to fully participate in it, do anything with it or for it.

This is the situation which is sprouting Catholic undergrounds that I spoke of in the ministry piece; people decide to walk out of the parochial structure and form a free congregation. There is one such group in Washington. Such a situation is still defined largely by alienation, however, and is feeding a lot off its tears for its bread. There is no clean solution. It is the betwixt and between of a *kairos*. My general feeling, however, as this has worked itself out in my existential development, is that we have to get somewhere where we can do something. To exist in a situation of frustration, on the fringes, the future blocked, no hope of participation or contribution ultimately turned out not to be a good matrix for the maturation of the self. It is soul destroying; it is not well taken into some notion of penance or discipline, because real mortification is creative, self-releasing, freeing, and hopeless frustration is not life-giving.

This is why I no longer make my local church a Roman parish, but an ecumenical Episcopal parish. I have no intentions of "joining" the Episcopal church, and no one wants me to. But it is a place where I can be in a community that I can

17. Rosemary Ruether, "Post-Ecumenical Christianity," in *Ecumenist* 5, no. 1 (November–December 1966): 3–7, which was reprinted as Chapter 8 of *The Church against Itself*.

believe in, among people who have a common faith with me, where I can participate and have a communal being, where I can contribute something and where my contribution is valued. Yet this does not alter my identity with, concern for historic Roman Catholicism. I have here a community, a community of friendship, a pulpit through the press, a community within the community commonly devoted to the reform of the Roman Catholic branch of the historical church, but I do not have a local church with Roman Catholics. In the most fundamental expression of the church, I do not gather with them, except in so far as the Underground Catholics themselves gather with me at St. Stephen's. It is unhappy, but there is no other possible solution. Fringe existence in the dead parochial structure proved to be too soul destructive, participatory existence in the underground too tiresome and basically unproductive because unreal, lacking any objective "place," i.e., bit of matter, if you will, to be redeemed. Charismatic community and institutional or historical setting have to relate in order to get a productive situation. Dead institution alone, charismatic community unrelated and therefore irresponsible to the historical task isn't it. You have to work with institutions. That is the historical condition under which the eschatological community exists, but you have to find a niche (or create a niche) where a part of the institution has some minimum hope of entering the revolution. It is not a question of being a groovy people. St. Stephen's doubtless looks very groovy to outsiders. To us who are it, we know that we have just begun to get underway, but we are underway, that is the important thing. We are not alienated, frustrated, fringe people over against powers that be, we are the powers that be, we are underway together, and our limitations are the limitations of our lack of insight, imagination, etc. The future ceases to be blocked, the road opens up ahead, the soul expands, not in a paltry sense of egoism, but in the sense of a plant with a place to flower. It's fun, it's good. It is still sad and unhappy that I cannot do this in and for a Roman parochial structure, but there is no such Roman parochial structure anywhere within reach. To hang on to a structure where the future is blocked is not right where there is a real alternative, but the alternative is not necessarily clean cut, or without pain to what is left behind. One can only work where one can and hope that these various parts of one intentionality will converge at some new point beyond the present. That's the best that I can do at this point. I can't tell you what is the best that you can do at this point. The same principles that apply to parochial community apply to monastery. Although we have talked of special "roles" of monastery, function of service for the whole church, being an "academia" of retreat and reflection, and these are surely things that they could do, basically monastery is not any of these things, but simply church — being the church, being the eschatological community under the conditions of historical existence. That is why my description of church (which I wrote as a description of St. Stephen's) struck you as monastic theology. It is, or rather monastic self-understanding is, simply and nothing else than ecclesia. This becomes the more evident as we leave the Constantinian era behind (which produced monasticism as the authentic expression of church when local church ceased to be eschatological community and became the religious expression of society at large), and parochial structure ceases to be hereditary and becomes more and more voluntary, more and more gathered community, monastic theology and theology of local church reconverge. Should you remain committed to that local church known as Abbey of Gethsemani, or should you look for another? No possibility of answering that until there is in fact another about which one can weigh the values. Frustration but love and loyalty, on the one hand, but until you have something in the other hand about which you can say, "pain of departure, construed disloyalty, but a chance to be, to make a contribution, to have the road block removed, the future opened up" there is nothing to weigh. Obviously that doesn't happen abstractly. It happens concretely, not as an abstract possibility but as a concrete, real possibility, as "X" community which is ready to be on the way. Pain of leaving something behind, but also a faint hope or possibility that only if some forge out to something new will the rest have a new place towards which to move. Some people must create a new place to stand, a new possibility before the rest can have a new horizon. An *avante garde* is an *avante* for the sake of leading the rest, not leaving them behind. That doesn't mean that the freer, more *avante* situation is so great, there is only a relative not an absolute difference between it and the deader community, but after all the difference between a haircut and a decapitation is also only a relative difference, but it is a relative difference which, from the point of view of personal existence, can become tantamount to an absolute difference, a possibility to be, over against a lack of possibility to be. A relative difference that may mean a possibility of making some fuller contribution is not to be despised because it is not yet heaven, because it is still subject to the same ambiguity, the same tedious dialectic of charisma and institution that is the lot of the eschatological community in history. Please don't be put off by my barren style. The passion that is behind these structures, for the time being, needs to be stripped away, because I am trying to get the correct relations here. I am more interested in trying to get that clearly then to decorate it with the passion, anger and love that is all over it as the flesh and blood of this structure.

Enclosed is a little St. Stephen'inalia you might be interested to read. The image article was originally written on the specific application of disposable art[18] and was followed up by an article describing the putting into practice of this concept of the church's culture as "disposable art" at St. Stephen's. It will appear in the *Living Light*.[19] I'll send you a copy when it comes out. I am

18. Rosemary Ruether, "Visual Arts for the Church of the Present and Future," *Living Light* 4, no. 2 (Summer 1967): 84–93.

19. Rosemary Ruether, "St. Stephen's Educational Program," *Living Light* 5, no. 1 (Spring 1968): 30–43.

not trying to suggest any specific application for you. You have to make that. I am obviously trying to say something about comparative communities, some of which have possibilities for moving and where one can have a future in it, and places which may not and from which it may be better to depart in order to suggest to them, too, a new possibility which they will not be able to see until you go ahead and do it.

Best,
Rosemary

P.S. Do you save letters, and do you have any way of duplicating them? In the first two letters of this correspondence, beginning on response to your letter of January 29, I wrote some stuff on scripture, Jesus, Christology, etc., and now I would like to see what it was that I said. I am really stupid not to put a carbon in when I am working out an idea in a letter, but that is something that I never think about ahead of time.

❧❧

April 9, 1967

Dear Rosemary:

*I*t is a Sunday evening and, because the community has its day of recollection, I have had the day off (no conference to give). Have thought a lot, and straight I think, and got in the sun, and am in my right mind, and have now reread your letter again: it is very dense and tight and solid. It is very good to have you coming right through and no need to be defensive and perplexed about it. Helps me to be straight too. Do you know the little magazine *Scandalon?* In the second number there is a splendid summation of the kind of thing you are talking about (busting off from the institution and getting in the charismatic community). I will send it if you have not seen it already. Tell me. Do I know your Fr. William Jerr? Seems familiar. The Lexington Seminary people used to come over here, and we used to talk. I am out of that now, however.

You are right about the alienation bit. I think that is my own problem. To be a hermit without insisting on being "alienated." As if I needed alienation as an excuse. It is a way of chickening out on the charism, that I really think my problem is simply that of being a hermit and not making a fuss about it. Of being without support and not complaining. Whether or not it means leaving this particular institution is not the issue at the moment. I have left it, as far as the practical conduct of my life is concerned (apart from things like laundry and food: like being on relief though). I think the thing is really that I must stand on my own feet for real and work out the relation of my life with, for instance, yours on a much deeper and more mature level. Without institutional justification. Without being in the groovy group and so on (not calling your group groovy). And maintaining the friendships and contacts I have. Poets and so on. If later it turns out that it is still a sham, my being a hermit and staying here, then the solution will also show. Right now I just don't see that part of it. What has come clear is that for the last year I have been shilly shallying around with the solitude part of it without realizing that that was what I was up to. That is why the community issue is for me at the moment a confusion and a temptation that is beside the point.

I am, at the moment, terribly suspicious of all monastic "solutions." They all seem to me to be as phony or more phony than the status quo. If I seek another Church it must be another honest monastic group: and there is one, started by a former novice of mine [Ernesto Cardenal], in Latin America. He wants me there, but it is impossible to do it legally and not the *kairos* for a revolutionary break. At least that is how it looks today.

I have begun working over the old monastic literature again and, really, the events in Egypt at the end of the 4th century are shocking. A dreadful business. And yet there was so much truth in some of those old guys in the desert. Did you ever see my little book on the Sayings of the Fathers? I'll send it if you like.

If you want a copy of that letter, I'll get Dan Berrigan to have one made and give it to him next time he comes. People don't mind their own business around here. You really should keep carbons. Thanks for your letter. I understand you now, and I'm right with you. The little account of the liturgy is most moving. Dan Berrigan and I celebrated one of those Episcopal liturgies here together quietly out of sight one day. Not at all like you had though.

I don't think I am rationalizing or evading when I say I think I owe it to you to pursue my own way and stand on my own in this sort of marginal and lost position I have. I am sometimes terribly hit by its meaning which is something I just cannot explain, because it is something you are not supposed to explain and must get along without explaining.

> With my love,
> *Tom*

❧

Dear Thomas:

*B*ill Jerr was with the Lexington group and remembers you very fondly. I told him I didn't know what was with you, whether you were in a serious crisis or not, and he said not to worry about you, you were always having crises anyway, and he couldn't imagine you any place else but Gethsemani, so ... so much for you. He also said you were "real soul," which is just about the highest compliment we have around here.

I still think it would be great if you could be relating in an integral way with some situation. I can imagine some kind of real free maverick monastic set up with you as a sort of elder states-man and idea man, i.e., free, yet not over against the set up, but a leading spirit for it. Father Wendt kind of runs St. Stephen's that way. He never administers anything. He sort of roves around sparking ideas, and everybody else works like a dog for him, but all on their own initiative. There are no committees or organizations; it is the most disorganized place in the world, and twenty times more things get done than any place else. Everybody loves each other like mad, and that is why they work so hard. I have never done so much work for a church in my life as the 10 months I have been there. But that kind of situation can't be manufactured. It just sort of gets given to you. Right now I am probably so gassed by the new experience of being loved by a community instead of hated, that I hate to see anybody else in a marginal situation.

Come on in, the water's fine. No, sorry, for some reason I prefer my tree top.

I sort of have a different problem though, of having too many people wanting me to play games in their camp, feeling a responsibility in various directions, not knowing quite how to parcel out my identity over these various commitments. As I get more and more deeply embraced by St. Stephen's, get sent as their representative for the Consultation on Church Union, get asked as their parish *Peritus* to talk at other Episcopal parishes, it becomes difficult to keep explaining that I am not an Episcopalian. On the other hand, I am writing more and more as a Catholic in the Catholic press, and this increasing role throws the balance more into jeopardy. Also the Catholic underground wants me to travel and play their church games. We just have to keep hammering away at a whole new concept of Christian commitment out beyond these structures, relating freely to whatever parts of them you can contribute to, in whatever combination arises and resist the totalizing demands of the denominational identity as a thing of the past. This style is becoming more common. I have had a lot of letters from people beginning to embark on this road, and even some of the Romans who work with the People's mass also make their local neighborhood community somewhere else, in this case a kind of very free Lutheran parish run out of a basement called the Community of Christ. I think I have to keep on working out the theological and ecclesial understanding of this new situation, because it seems to me that the more people can begin to see and understand the meaning of this new possibility, the more we can begin to really overcome the schisms of the past, and we have an ecumenism built on a rising of a new church beyond these schisms, and not a corporation merger from the top. We have to really begin to get to work to alter the currency so that these bloody structures stop destroying people's souls by equating the rules with these structures as though they represented some absolute. We should neither obey them nor disobey them, but move out into a new and more authentic possibility. I think that is what you are working on in your context too.

Love,
Rosemary

P.S. What do you mean by "one of those Episcopal liturgies"? I have your book on the Fathers and do especially like the shaggy old desert Father.

❈

May 5, 1967

Dear Rosemary:

Sorry for the long delay in answering this time. I have had publishers here and lawyers here and visiting firemen — if you think I live in utter isolation you are quite wrong. I wish I had a little more of it sometimes. But the letters have been held up. Some day I ought to try to see what it is like to be really out of communication and isolated. Just to see what it is like. Not as a permanent thing, because I don't think that is important. But in other words, a hermit today is not all that isolated, with letters, planes coming down this way, and so on. I think I am probably much more in communication with people all over the place, all over the world, than most active lifers are. So much for the treetop; but I don't deny the water sounds fine where you are. I was sure I recognized Bill Jerr. Give him my regards.

Like you, hermit and all, I find myself tugged this way and that by various groups wanting me to get into their games, if only remotely. I think that we both have to come to terms with the problem of overload, in many different spheres. Work, engagement, study, out speaking, games. It seems to take a mixture of charismatic flexibility and of dogged common sense. And a point at which one becomes known for saying "No" if not "Nuts." It seems to me that the business of knee jerk response to every invitation is even worse than being holed up in some sort of mossy conservatism that refuses to move. Not worse, but in a way it can be more destructive and meaningless. A lot of this stuff just has to roll off like water off a duck's back. In the end they even forget they asked you. In fact, the whole issue itself is forgotten after a week.

My way is to be notoriously off beat and inconsistent, but to be able to establish a kind of consistency within the off beatness, which people gradually come to recognize and respect. With preference for the personal contact bit. Like I am more ready to get in some personal involvement (by mail) with some specific Snick [Student Non-Violent Coordinating Committee] people than to sign some declaration in general. And I like to keep my freedom to get mixed up more in poetic causes than in liberal stereotype shows. And so on. With these supposed principles, I do however make a lot of mistakes and say more than I should, but it doesn't matter, there is so much silly noise anyway. But I think I have learned to say "No" better than I did ten years ago, or six (ten years ago I didn't have that many chances to get asked). What I do absolutely agree with is the need to be free from a sort of denominational tag. Though I have one in theory (people still have me categorized in terms of *The Seven Storey Mountain*), I am really not any of the things they think, and I don't comfortably wear the label of monk either, because I am now convinced that the first way to be a decent monk is to be a non-monk and an anti-monk, as far as the "image" goes: but I am certainly quite definite about wanting to stay in the bushes (provided I can make some sort of noises that will reach my offbeat friends).

Now for a serious idea: Let's you and I figure out some way we can do a dialogue for this magazine in England (see enclosed mimeo of my Easter blat). Perhaps something on what I have just been saying, but also what we have been saying about monasticism. Something about where are the real monks and so on. What would be the best way to do it without getting it rambling over the whole landscape? Letters and then edit the stuff? Or you get down this way some time and we could do it on tape? That would have to be in the fall I expect. Have you some ideas? I could send along an example of the kind of thing they have done if you like. Please let me know. By the way I have been meaning to say how much I liked your piece on divorce in the *Catholic World*[20] and also the bit on DuBay's CIO in *Continuum*.[21]

Love,
Tom

---

20. This article is more readily available in *Commonweal:* Rosemary Ruether, "Divorce No Longer Unthinkable," *Commonweal* 86, no. 4 (April 14, 1967): 117–19, 122.
21. Rosemary Ruether, "Father DuBay and the Priests' Union," *Continuum* 5, no. 1 (Spring 1967): 182–84. Father DuBay attempted to establish a union among the priests to safeguard their rights against the hierarchy. This attempt embroiled him in a fierce battle in his own archdiocese, Los Angeles, with Cardinal McIntyre.

Dear Friends:[22]

*I*t has been a beautiful warm Easter here, though the most recent news from the East Coast complains of much snow. Jim
Forest wrote from his CPF [Catholic Peace Fellowship] office
in Nyack that he felt like Dr. Zhivago in Siberia, and Adri-
enne Mariani had some amusing suggestions about what might
be done to discourage the ground hog from sticking his head
out and being confronted with despair. Actually, however, it was
eighty all afternoon here on Holy Saturday and sixty at one thirty
a.m. when I got back to my cell after the Easter Vigil.

Answering letters individually gets to be more and more of a
problem. Not that I am pitying myself, but just to give new correspondents some idea of why I simply cannot answer letters most
of the time. Besides my ordinary work, I now have on my desk
the following: One complete manuscript of a novel on which I
am asked to comment by a publisher. A set of galleys of a book on
Zen, ditto. Several chapters of a book on mysticism to read and
criticize. A long statement of the Vietnam War I am supposed
to sign (generally I don't sign any of these statements, because I
can't read the papers or watch TV to keep up as others do). A list
of twenty-four magazine articles which I must either read and
report on myself, or get others to summarize, for the magazine
of the Order. A book review article of six or seven books about
Camus, in state of outline, to be written somehow in the next
week or so. At least two books to review for the magazine of the
Order. (I mention only the two that happen to be directly visi-
ble at the moment. There are probably others on the shelf behind
me or buried under the mass of other material that confronts me.)
Finally, on top of that, I have an urgent report to write on an official matter, and am requested to give this top priority. And so on.
The life of a writing hermit is certainly not one of lying around in

---

22. This is the second form letter that Merton sent to Ruether.

the sun or of pious navel gazing. Nevertheless there is the question of meditation which, to me, is always the first thing of all, because without it the rest becomes meaningless. In such circumstances, writing letters, receiving visits, and so on, would simply complicate matters beyond all reasonable measure. Yet, I do, of course, have to answer business mail, urgent requests, questions from people in a state of crisis, and all that. Carrying on an ordinary friendly correspondence is normally just out of the question. Note also that I have no secretary for correspondence, and that it is increasingly difficult to find someone in the monastery to type manuscripts. (I am most grateful to the ones who are helping me in this matter, both inside and outside the monastery.)

I recommend a very interesting and important new magazine which is being published at Cambridge (England). The first issues have just reached me. It is called *Theoria to Theory,* and the purpose is to get some lively dialogue going between theologians and contemplatives on one hand, and secular scientists, philosophers, and humanists, on the other. It is the most promising new venture of its kind that I have seen. It is edited by Anglicans and is more informal and free wheeling than the new Roman Catholic publications, which still strike me as too formal and still a bit triumphalist. (There is, of course, a new aggressive triumphalism of the left just as there is an old stuffy triumphalism of the right.) Part of the editorial in the first issue reads as follows: "To those who ... still hope there might be something in Christianity, or indeed in any other religion, we would simply say: Things aren't as hopeless as you might think. There are more things in heaven and earth than are dreamt of in any of the philosophies currently in use. *Nil illegitime carborundum,* which is hot dog Latin for, "Don't let the bastards grind you down." The magazine can be obtained from 9 Marion Close, Cambridge, England.

A friend wrote quoting a line of verse: "In the juvenescence of the year comes Christ the Tiger" and wondered if Easter was going to be like that. There is an inner strength which is "ours" yet "not ours," which can be for us or against us, depending on whether we decide to face it and submit, or seek to evade and resist it. Easter is the season of that strength (and Easter is all year round, really). At Easter we resolve liturgically and communally to "face it" and to join this Tiger who is then our Tiger and our Lamb. (I am thinking of the two great Blake poems: "Tyger Tyger burning bright....") There is no joy but in the victory of Christ over death in us: and all love that is valid has something of that victory. But the power of love cannot "win" in us if we insist on opposing it with something else to which we can cling, on which we trust because we ourselves can manipulate it. It all depends who is in control: our own ego, or Christ. We must learn to surrender our ego-mastery to His mastery. And this implies a certain independence even of apparently holy systems and routines, official "answers" and infallible gimmicks of every kind. Easter celebrates the victory of love over everything. *Amor vincet omnia.* If we believe it we will understand it, because belief is what opens the door to love. But to believe only in systems and *statements* and not in *people* is an evasion, a betrayal of love. When we really believe as Christians, we find ourselves trusting and accepting *people* as well as dogmas. Woe to us when we are merely orthodox, and reject human beings, flesh and blood, the aspirations, joys and needs of men. Yet there is no fruit, either, in merely sentimental gestures of communion that mean little, and seek only to flatter or placate. Love can also be tough and uncompromising in its fidelity to its own highest principles. Let us be united in joy, peace and prayer this Easter and always. "Fear not" says Jesus. "It is I. I am with you all days!..."

All my love, in Christ,
Thomas Merton

My Campaign Platform[23]
for non-Abbot and permanent keeper of present doghouse.

My Dear Brethren:

I realize that you are for the most part sane enough not to vote for a dope like me, but since there seems to be still a certain amount of confusion in some minds, I hope you will excuse me for referring to such an indelicate matter. It may be worth while to set down in unmistakenly clear terms exactly what my position is. Just in case anyone is interested.

1. More than ten years ago I made a private vow never to accept an Abbatial election. This vow was approved by Dom James and the Abbot General, Dom Gabriel Sortais, both of whom accepted it with evident relief as a sign of the Lord's mercy and of His continued determination to protect the Order from disaster. I consider myself permanently bound by this vow and believe that under no circumstances should I consent to a dispensation.

2. My reasons:

(a) My vocation is to the solitary life plus a certain amount of writing. Indications have long since made it morally certain that this is what our Lord asks of me. To accept the Abbatial office and dignity would be an infidelity to my true calling.

(b) I would be completely incapable of assuming the duties of a superior, since I am in no sense an administrator still less a business man. Nor am I equipped to spend the rest of my life arguing about complete trivialities with one hundred and twenty-five slightly confused and anxiety ridden monks. The responsibility of presiding over anything larger than a small chicken coop is beyond my mental, moral and physical capacities.

(c) Even if I did once cherish a few ideas about possibilities of monastic development, these have by now become foggy

---

23. This was sent to Ruether along with Merton's form letter for Easter.

and indistinct, due to the encroachments of age and mental deterioration. In any case I always knew that *nothing* I might be interested in could be accomplished in a large, well established and highly official institution.

(d) Since I have been a constant and unfailing disedification to the community for twenty-six years, it is obvious that anyone voting for me would have to be in a dubious condition spiritually. You would probably be voting for me on the grounds that I would grant you plenty of beer. Well, I would, but it takes more than that to make a good Abbot.

(e) I cannot think of any single thing connected with the office of Abbot that makes any real sense to me in the context of my own life.

3. Consequently — in all seriousness — I feel obligated in conscience to do everything in my power to prevent this happening and to refuse it if it happens. I cannot under any circumstances agree that I should accept an election as Abbot. My vow and my solitary life are the divine will for me.

4. I apologize once again for putting something like this on paper, but it would be even more embarrassing to have to talk about it *viva voce*. And of course I do realize that the matter is not that urgent: few would be tempted to waste their votes on me in any case. If you threw the paper away without reading it, you missed nothing. If you got this far without feeling physically indisposed, pray for me. Otherwise, see Fr. Eudes — and pray for me anyhow. *Tu autem Domine miserere nobis* (note conservative trend!)

Your brother in Christ,
br m louis

Dear Thomas:

*S*top protesting! You don't have to justify your life!!! I think that is why I keep needling you, because I figure if you have to keep justifying there must be something wrong — towards which this dialogue involves me in some responsibility — so much for that.

I like your idea of a dialogue on monasticism although I see it as a complicated one since we shall not be speaking as though detached from our existential situations. I think I would prefer to work out some of the things I have been trying to say about the eschatological principle in the church and how this is expressing itself today and how this is related to monasticism as a traditional expression of this dimension of the church. If you want to have some taped exchange, that might be possible too. I will be giving a talk at the Grail the 20th of August, and then I will go to Oberlin in Ohio for a Kent conference, where I am also giving a paper; that takes me up through the weekend — we might come down through your way either before or after that time — Herc's family lives in Cincinnati, which (with my inadequate knowledge of geography inside the two coasts of this country) I take to be not too far away from your neck of the woods.

You are right about the pressure to play all kinds of games. Right now I experience that less in the form of requests for talks, because I am gay enough to enjoy tripping around and talking to all kinds of people, but in the form of pressure to write books. The requests to write things in book form I find a kind of invasion of my creative privacy — I want to write a book as a real expression of how I am developing and not to write something until I have completed a kind of new phase of development, that will really be a new contribution. To be asked to write according to some pre-fab topic of a publisher, to have publishers try to tie up your writing in advance is a bag that I really want to climb out of. Perhaps you can help me here, I don't really understand this publisher's bit about insisting that they have a line on your next book once you sign a contract with them for a previous one. What is that all about? I don't feel like having such invisible liens on my typewriter. I have a "don't write me, I'll write you" approach to publishers, which, I suppose, is all very unprofessional.

I enclose a little piece about our Pentecost Happening. Do you know Joe Wise? He is a Roman Catholic, lay theologian and musician — one of the real creative ones, I think. He did the music at the Liturgical conference for St. Steve's last fall. We are all going to make paper vestments so everyone will have a festive garb for the Eucharist. Polly Evans, the wife of one of the priests, made an Easter vestment that is the most psychedelic thing you have ever seen, bright orange with big flowers in hot pinks, reds, etc., so we will use that as the main vestment with everybody else in whatever mad garb they dream up at the be-in — last Sunday everybody wrote Pentecost messages and stuffed them in the balloons to send up over the city on Sunday. Some of the messages were pretty rare, especially from the children. My son David persisted in seeing the whole thing as an air attack on the city and writing things like "surrender now, or we will bomb." The messages also had a printed message with Pentecost greetings, so presumably such additions won't panic the city. I kind of like the idea of the Holy Ghost as an air attack on the city; it fits in quite well with the apocalyptic description of Pentecost in Acts, i.e., the redeemed corrective of man's word — surrender now or — is God's Word, "repent now, for the Kingdom of God is at hand.

Love,
Rosemary

Dear Rosemary:

I know *Theoria to Theory* would like a dialogue, as they have confirmed this. How to do it, and about what: I am not deep enough in eschatology to keep up with you on that perhaps. We'll see. I think we ought to wait with the actual "publishable" stuff and just talk without any afterthought of using what we say. Yes, this is about two hundred miles from Cincinnati. If you are down in Cincinnati it would not be hard to get here as there are good new roads (via Lexington). Would enjoy seeing you. As I say, let's think in terms of just talking and not of publishing what we say at this juncture.

About publishers: the normal practice is for them to take first option on your next book. All that means is that they have a right to get first look at whatever you write next. If they choose to suggest what you ought to write next, that is their affair, but you are under no obligation whatever to say anything but "nuts." I usually tell them that their suggestions don't interest me. That I am doing something else. That I couldn't do the damn fool thing they have suggested if my life depended on it, etc., etc. Thus one preserves a certain amount of independence. It is the worst thing a writer can do, to get caught up on some publisher's little team of moneymakers for the here and now: involved in what is thought to be actual at the moment by a little in group of publishers, editors and so on. I'd say avoid that like the plague, it will do you no good whatever.

I liked your Pentecost thing and hope it went off well. Your David had a good idea in his balloon message. On Pentecost I went to Dan Walsh's ordination and concelebrated in my own stumbling way. After which I got stoned on champagne.

There is supposed to be an exhibition of some far out drawings of mine in Washington and I told the man if anyone was mad enough to buy one the money should go to your Church. But I haven't heard a thing from him and don't know what is happening. You mention Joe Wise. The name rings a bell, but I don't think I have ever met him. Or maybe a long time ago, like at College??

One really lovely thing you should see if you are down this way is the old Shaker place near Lexington. I think they have a guest house now, and one can even stay there. One thing eschatology seems to have done for them: it was connected with marvelous work with their hands. That strikes me as something very real!

Best always,

Love,
Tom

June 29, 1967

Dear [Tom]:[24]

*T*his is a letter about a family I have gotten to know this year in Washington. Wanda and Billie Parks grew up in the District of Columbia. Wanda went to school in the old Southwest section before it was cleared for urban redevelopment, and the people who lived there before could no longer afford the new apartments. Wanda went to school until she was sixteen, and when she gave back her books and told the teachers that she had had enough, her ability to read, write, and spell was still minimal, although she is normally intelligent. Billie worked as a fruit packer, and the Parks children began to arrive at regular yearly intervals. One day as Billie walked home with his meager pay check, he was jumped, his pay check taken, and he was left with

---

24. This is the first form letter that Ruether sent to Merton; both of them frequently refer to its contents. Ruether wrote an article about this family. Their name was changed to protect their identity at the time: "The Larkes and the Changing Seasons," *National Catholic Reporter* 4, no. 47 (September 25, 1968): 12.

slashed wrists that incapacitated him for further manual labor. The family went on welfare. Three years ago when they were unable to pay their rent, they were set out on the street and lost all their possessions. Wanda has never been able to replace any of the furniture or household goods, and is still cooking without real dishes or pots and pans. The family then moved into a one room basement apartment about 15 by 18 feet in size. A dark narrow alley runs behind the room, and here the family cooks and eats. This has been their home for three years. This year two of the children who had been living with relatives had to return home and the effort to house eight people in this space proved impossible. A small extra room was rented upstairs, raising the rent to $100. The children are thin and under-nourished, look several years younger than their age and are constantly ill with colds and infections. Yet Wanda prefers to keep them indoors much of the time rather than risk the danger of the streets. Efforts to secure improved housing were discouraging. The total family welfare check comes to $254; after $100 rent, $84 for food stamps, $15 for bus tickets, there is not much left for other basic necessities. The food stamps do not provide a good diet and run out before the end of the month, and so Wanda resorts to the church for canned goods and other staples. Clothing is mostly found in second hand stores or at the "flea market" run by the church. Wanda does a lot of volunteer work for the church, but she has to be careful about any paid work since extra income will be deducted from her check. She also has to be careful about gifts because welfare clients are not supposed to possess any "luxury items" and "luxury items" include any electrical appliances including fans (do you have any idea what it is like to live with 8 people in one room through a Washington summer?). When the last baby was born, a friend gave Wanda a small diaper washer that was electric and the case worker took it away because it was a "luxury item."

The church has become an important center for the family since a friend took her there following the eviction, and Wanda does not want to move out of the Cardoza area within walking distance of St. Stephen and the Incarnation, but this part of town, like most center city slums, is an expensive place to live, even for poor people. The paper lists two bedroom apartments in this area for under $100, but they always say "no children." After much hunting, Wanda and friends from the church have recently found a small three bedroom house not too far away that rents for $97.50 and will take the children. To get it she has to put up $150 but she has already paid the July rent and does not have the $50 security deposit. The house has the space she needs, and it is on a less hostile street than her present place, but the insides are in deplorable condition. A muddy pink paint covers the walls sprayed right over the filth of innumerable tenants. The floors sag and are incrusted with dirt.

We think it would be great if this could be the time for a whole new start for Wanda and Billie, for Barbara 13, John 11, Ralph 10, Linda 8, little Billie 7, and Connie age 3. To do this we need a little money. We need some money to get this house. Then we need some money for paint and plaster and things like that. Then we need a little more to get some household goods. We have a lot of people who would be willing to work, but we don't have much money. Would you like to help by sending a contribution to Rosemary Ruether, c/o St. Stephen and the Incarnation, 16th and Newton Streets, N.W., Washington, D.C.

Sincerely,
Rosemary Ruether

P.S. [addressed to Merton] Maybe you know someone you could pass this on to —

Dear Rosemary:

*T*hanks for your letter — and the more recent mimeographed letter too. I showed this to Fr. Abbot and asked if we could not contribute something, so here is a small check. It is not much but it is something. That kind of situation is just horrible, and people forget that there are millions of others that have to cope with it. I don't know if any drawings have been sold. I am not sure whether the exhibit is still on. I haven't heard anything. It was supposed to be at 3723 S. St. NW, a place called, of all things, the Fun House, which sounds strange. But it is run by a poet called John Pauker and his wife and the fun as far as I can understand is a matter only of the arts.

Let's keep thinking of the possibility of your stopping here late in August, and maybe talking a bit. You ask about the hippies and from what I know of them the idea sounds good, attractive, and also pathetic. I can't judge because I haven't seen them and this is something one needs to *see* all right, and I guess touch, etc. One can't judge without being all wound up in that for a while. Thirty years ago my friends and I were to some extent doing that, though not so colorfully and I guess we were as much beat as hip, but there was a sort of millennial feeling about it too: but we were not that much of a group, just four or five of us really, living in the woods in upstate NY. Some kids in California, though, have written asking me to write for "an underground paper" they are starting. It sounds most innocent and as you say full of grace, but yet one does not get the feeling that they are very happy. Four or five years ago I ran into one such movement in Latin America, and have kept in contact, and they seem more positive, and there are some good writers among them too. I guess though they will gravitate more and more toward Cuba... one of them just wrote she was going there to work this summer. But the Cubans I know *in* Cuba aren't very happy either.

I will pass your letter on, the one about the Parks family, and I do hope you succeed in getting them out of the crisis and at least relatively comfortable. And fed, and clothed, and all that they need. I finally got a sink in my place so I don't have to wash dishes in a bucket on the floor... or in the rain bucket outside, but I still can't drink the water here, have to carry it up from the monastery.

Keep well, have a good summer,
Love,
Tom

✻✿✻

July 10, 1967

Dear Rosemary:[25]

I just heard today about the exhibit of drawings: two have been sold so far and there is money waiting for you there. I wrote to them and said you would present yourself in one way or other to claim the loot. You will know best what to do with it, like whether for the Parks family or others in the same fix.

The exhibit sounds like fun and you might like it: has some interesting welding done by Negro kids in a reform school or something. I wish I could see it all. Some of my drawings have been framed by them in a way that sounds to me quite baroque, so I don't vouch for that part of it. The simpler frames I chose here for the earlier set are fairly effective.

Would the parish like a drawing? If so, choose one. I'd be delighted to be "present" at St. Stephen and Incarnation in the form of a calligraphy.

Best always and blessings and love,
Tom

---

25. Three phrases were pasted on this letter. They had apparently been clipped from a newspaper or magazine and said, "The Monks. Modern Moving...with Old Fashioned Care." It was not Merton's usual style to decorate his letters.

Dear Thomas:

I am most appreciative of your help with the Parks. I have gotten enough help to be able to do a pretty good redoing on
the house and gifts of furniture and household goods to fit it out
decently. I hope to have enough left over to put in a little brick
patio in what is presently a mud swamp in the back. We can get
some sand fill and used brick and lay it in, just a small area behind
between the alley and the opposite tenements; we can dig a small
tree up from a nearby forest and stick it in there and change the
scenery a bit. Mrs. Parks has a certain amount of get up and go,
too bad she has to carry around Billy on her back, who is basically
a bum riding along on his hard luck. The important thing is the
children for whom the future is not yet closed.

When you mentioned your bucket and rain water it reminded
me of a theme that I would like to work on some more. I call
it "the Poverty hang-up in Christian thought." It applies to you
living in a primitive way in the woods and the Miller and other
Catholic Worker types living in the urban ghetto level in the
city. But what does it really mean? In actuality you only share
the external appearances of economic deprivation with the poor
hillsman who has no running water, and they likewise with the
ghetto poor. But actually there is nothing in common between
you and them for the simple reason that they have to be there,
and you don't. You can dress up and walk into a hotel, and they
won't throw you out. You have the knowledge and skill to handle the larger world of our society, and that is precisely what they
lack. No one would really confuse a Catholic Worker type with
a real ghetto person, and no one would really confuse you with a
real impoverished hillbilly. You may identify with them, but they
do not identify with you. The reason is that you can never share

the culture of poverty, the deprivation of outlook, and because you don't share this, however much you may ape the external circumstances of poverty, your culture marks you off as a member of the possessing class. We have a very firm class stratification, perhaps even hardening today. The ladder upward is education. If you make it on the educational ladder you can move up, but those who have parents who have already made it have the running start. Why identify with poverty then? There are alternative rationales. One tends to fall over into a kind of pragmatism. I want to simplify my existence, have to do with a minimum of confusion, involvement, etc. Most of the time the pragmatic rationale seems to be the one you use. There is the more idealistic rationale. Live insecurely, live a life of witness against injustice, live where poor people are so you can help them. Catholic Worker types fuse together these kinds of idealistic rationale. But there is a fatal contradiction between simultaneously idealizing poverty and working to overcome other people's poverty, presumably so they can stop being poor and start being modestly affluent. A third kind of rationale adheres in both of these, but goes beyond them. Poverty somehow points to the Kingdom, when people will live in a kind of effortless fashion, but suppose the Kingdom never comes? Suppose it is just a wish projection of our ideals of what the good life would be like? If the Kingdom never comes, then perhaps we should stop living quixotically in an "as if" fashion and get to work remaking the face of the earth here and now. The Jews remained an impoverished hated people as long as they waited for the Messiah to conquer the promised land for them. Now they have stopped waiting for a mythical Messiah and started being their own Messiah and conquering the promised land for themselves. That's more than they got before by being poor and pious. It is an interesting and long lived hang-up, but I can't make head nor tail out of it.

The below is a conversation between me and Marshall and David Lee recorded as I painted on a sash in the slum house, and Marshall and David, ages 5 and 7 respectively, who live on the same street, kick their heels on the mattress springs and make conversation.

"Hey, Rosemary. Will you let me paint?"

"Not today. I'll let you paint tomorrow when we get the tables here."

"I'm gonna be a painter man when I grow up. I'm gonna make a lot of money."

"What does your daddy do, Marshall?"

"My daddy's a construction worker. He'll give me anything I want. My mother doesn't want me to be no construction worker. She wants me to work in an of-fis."

(David) "My mother doesn't care about what I do. She doesn't want me to do nothing. She just tells me to get lost."

"Hey, Rosemary, you know the colored man's yell, 'hello baby,' at the white woman and the white woman, she gets maaaad!"

"Oh, really."

"The colored lady that lived in this house. She had a lot of kids and they didn't have no furniture or nothing. They just all slept on the floor on a bunch of dirty ole rags."

"My daddy beat up that colored lady. He told her if she comes around any more he is gonna kill her, that's what he said, he is gonna kill her. She had a boy friend named Clarence, and he beat her up. She had a lip sticking out like this (makes a mouth). The po-lice come and they say they is gonna take her to the hospital. But she say she don't have no money to go to no hospital."

"What happened to the lady?"

"Oh, they throwed her out. The lady lived here before that, they throwed her out too."

Love,
Rosemary

Dear Rosemary:[26]

I enjoyed your letter, especially the conversation. Those kids and those conversations! They are just beautiful. I am happy the Parks are getting in better shape and hope it won't all be censured as "luxury"!!

About your remarks on the poverty hangup. Good intuitions, and you raise some of the more urgent problems, the right *Problematik*. It is thorny. Yet, I think all such problems are harder to grasp now because everything has become slippery. We no longer have one unified set of ideas we start from: everything that we hold on the basis of one set of assumptions is questionable in terms of various other sets which remain open possibilities. For instance: there is a Christian vocation to voluntary poverty — because the poor are the eschatological people. So you do what you can to choose this eschatological lot, and try to be real about it knowing you won't entirely succeed. This presupposes a world in which "the poor are always with you." Suddenly a new eschatology shows up: it is possible to abolish poverty altogether. So then what do you do! Abolish it. But when we set about doing that, we find that we make poverty worse for the really poor, more inexorable, more hopeless, more grinding, more desperate. So then we see that there is yet another eschatological perspective: destroy the wicked society that is so full of contradictions.

One of my friends, a poet gal who lives in Mexico [Margaret Randall de Mondragón], solves it for herself by going to work in Cuba during the summer, cutting sugar cane, etc. Now in her case I don't think the identification is that phony at all, because what has happened is that the class hangup has been got rid of more or less. But then one is identifying not just with people, but also with a new institution. Thus the big problem, and again

---

26. This letter is decorated in the same manner as Merton's letter of July 10, 1967.

an eschatological problem, is the one that ends in choices of institutions over each other. Like you, I don't know. I think that the economic way out is full of traps, bigger and better than the others perhaps. You cite Israel: O.K.: Israel is a nation of westerners, an enclave of people from a tech civilization amid primitives who hate their guts and want to get rid of them at any price. The impact of Israel on the Near East has in fact resulted in zooming misery for hundreds of thousands of people. Of course it shouldn't have, but it did. And that is what I mean: the complexity and the mystery of human cussedness seems to set up inexorable blocks against our doing what we theoretically ought to be able to do.

So for my part, even though it is only a gesture and largely unreal (obviously I am not one of the hillbillies), I hang on in desperation to what I think I have been called to, trusting not in it but in the mercy of Christ who knows better than I that it isn't real, but that it is at least a choice. And there don't seem to be more meaningful ones around, for me, all things considered. So when I cite pragmatic reasons I am really being prudent and setting up what is a non-rationale, in order to avoid the institutional clichés, the monastery propaganda. I know, maybe I don't succeed.

In the monastery now there is a whole new dialog game going on, and they are trying to grapple with the poverty thing among other things. I don't see any way out for them, in this context. No matter which way they turn, they end up in nothing but games and gestures. I do agree with you that we have to start out with the very sobering realization that voluntary poverty, in the context of our society, cannot be anything but phony in so far as we are identified with the top layer of people anyway, like it or not. But the thing is, I think, to realize that this country is under judgement (it is Assyria, no?), and no matter where we go or what we do, we remain Assyrians who are under judgement. I think we have to start from there. Do you agree? And if so, what is it? What does it mean? The Ninevites fixed it by putting hairshirts on everyone including the cats and dogs. Is this practical? (Purely rhetorical question).

Love always,
Tom

P.S. How do you like my posh stationery — purely cynical in intent.

✿

c. July 20, 1967

Dear Thomas:

I have been in communication with John Pauker and shall go down to see the drawings sometime soon. We are working up a show of them at St. Stephen's at Father Wendt's suggestion. Probably a big to-do in September which will feature the drawings along with some very good metal sculpture being done at the local jail which John is interested in. Monks and jail birds...?

I got some very generous help on the Parks' new house, enough to do what I hoped for them as far as the living quarters go, so I expect whatever comes through from the drawings we will put into Father Wendt's discretionary fund from which he disburses to whoever is in need. We are having a great summer program here for the neighborhood children. Becky and David are also in it, but they are the only middle-class children and, except for the Parks, the only whiteys. They go to the theatre, do lots of dance and drama and arts and crafts, lots of trips, etc. — as the grand finale we are taking all 130 of them to Expo 67. Wild idea! We will charter a train and take everyone up for four days. The church is selling beer and crabs on Friday to finance the trip. Only Father Wendt would have had the bravado to think of doing something like that! I wish you could meet him.

I am trying to write a communion book for children for Herder and Herder, but it is not going well. I just don't really know if you can make the tradition hang together on the devastatingly simple level of children. The simple fact is that the Messiah hasn't come yet, and there is no getting around it. The whole edifice rests on a foundation of wishful thinking. Jesus has not risen from the dead, and we are still in our sins, to take up St. Paul's challenge. That's the bad news. Still and all, I believe. . . .

Best love,
Rosemary

P.S. I just got your poverty letter. Wow! all of a sudden you were cooking with gas! full of that kind of dark but full faith which is the only kind that I can really take . . . that was Luther's great genius, to understand the darkness of faith: sin bravely, but more bravely still believe. We walk not in achievement, but *fides sola*. Catholics have always so crudely and stupidly misunderstood what Luther was talking about here, partly because it is not a theology for beginners, but for those who have passed through everything, tried everything, put on every hair shirt and tried every kind of penitence and prayer and know the insufficiency of all of the efforts. He was a "graduated monk" too, you know, and his theology remains basically the result of his maturing in the monastic experience . . . even in the midst of his Kate and his ten kids. Destroy the evil society? or redeem the evil society? I am one of those mad Origenists who believe that when God is all in all, even the last enemy Satan will be redeemed. I believe in giving everyone, even the dogs, not hair shirts (which they already have), but flower power, baby.

Love
Rosemary

P.S. Enclosed is our St. Stephen's parish button.

August 4, 1967

Dear Rosemary:

*T*hanks for your note and the clippings — and also for your other letter. I was glad to hear about Fr. Wendt's action: it is good to see someone do something sane for once. As I see it, we are going to have to get used to a sort of climate of quasi-civil war that is not the kind we have in mind as the pattern for civil war (the war of the states), but really the kind of thing that went on in the religious wars of the seventeenth century — though perhaps without armies moving around. It will take sanity and patience and restraint and all that. For my part, I have suddenly got engrossed in a whole new line of study, a new approach (for me) — the anthropological one, the question of the clash between cultures (white and advanced with non-white and more or less primitive) which has produced all sorts of strange things by which people have tried to cope with the trauma. So I am involved in looking up eschatological cults in Africa, Melanesia, among American Indians, and so on. Very revealing I think. Am perhaps going to work with a psychiatrist friend on a book on violence, but probably not, as I am not a pro in that field. But still, I have the manuscript he has been doing, and it is absorbing too, and we will at least have a lot to say to each other. He worked with war criminals after the last war.

I guess all anyone can do is try to make sense out of his life. As to the Gospel side of it: I have always told Protestants coming around here that in my opinion a monk did not become a monk until he had gone through Luther's experience and knew that the monastic life was futile. To abandon the monastic life because it is futile is to seek justification by works. . . . No? Luther continued as a monk, as you say, and I have just reviewed a book by F. Parpert in German on this idea and on Evangelical monasticism. He says (and I agree) that perhaps the most contemplative-monastic people in the world today are the nuclear physicists (to me that means Bohr and the Copenhagen group who are my culture heroes).

One real problem for me keeps coming up. I get invited out of here to get in conferences of this or that for two or three days: something perfectly legitimate even in the books of some of the more conservative types in the Order. But my Abbot will not allow it under any circumstance. Even when it comes through channels. Like the Archbishop tried to get me out to meet with Cardinal Koenig in the east this summer (Cardinal Koenig can't come down here), but the Abbot blocks it anyway. He does not realize, I think, that his unconscious objective is to keep me out of sight and under wraps and, in a way, to shut me up. It is a form of silencing which he can resort to with what he thinks is a good conscience and "for my own good," when in fact it does deprive me of contacts and information and perspective. I try to tell him how wrong he is, but it does not get through. Ambivalent about it: on the one hand it makes me mad, for after all who wants to be castrated? But on the other hand these meetings and conferences do not amount to much, and one could get involved in an endless series of really stupid functions. In the end, I don't know. I know how the SNCC [Student Non-Violent Coordinating Committee] people feel.

Love,
Tom

Dear Thomas:

*T*he communion book is done.[27] After fretting over it for some time, all of a sudden it wrote itself. I think it will look very good with the graphic illustrations by Mary Jo [Huck]. When it is out I will send you a copy. My Gregory book is also nearing completion.[28] I have the proofs from Oxford. I think you might enjoy some parts of that, particularly his struggle between the "active" and the "contemplative" life, or as he calls it, the "philosophic life." I am very much interested in your interest in subcultures and eschatological revolution. I am going to be spending more time on that. I have a talk for the Kent-Danforth meeting on Barth's concept of chaos which I have been trying to use to apply to the theology of social apocalyptic revolution.[29] Next year I want to do a seminar at Howard on the theology of social change and look at the implied theology of the radical advocates of Black power (the white devil, etc.) and also the libertine utopia of the hippies. Both have good precedents in medieval Catholic history as you probably know.[30] My stand-by on this subject is Norman Cohn's *The Pursuit of the Millennium*. Would love to hear more of what you are doing in this area.

Pauker is working with us to do an art show in the Fall with your "signs" and his reformatory sculptures. At first we were a little worried about him, because he seemed to want to make

---

27. Rosemary Ruether, *Communion Is Life Together* (New York: Herder and Herder, 1968). Ruether subsequently wrote a companion volume entitled *Communion: A Parent-Teacher Manual* (New York: Herder and Herder, 1973).

28. Rosemary Ruether, *Gregory of Nazianzus, Rhetor and Philosopher* (Oxford: Clarendon Press, 1969). This was Ruether's doctoral dissertation.

29. This was subsequently published as Rosemary Ruether's "The Left Hand of God in the Theology of Karl Barth: Karl Barth as a Mythopoetic Theologian," *Journal of Religious Thought* 25, no. 1 (1968–69): 3–26.

30. Ruether's work in this area was subsequently published as *The Radical Kingdom: The Western Experience of Messianic Hope* (New York: Harper and Row, 1970).

a social killing on the show, but I think we understand each other now.

I am very puzzled by this relationship with your Abbot. It sounds very destructive for both of you. I really wonder that you don't go all the way with your present direction and really become a "free hermit." What does standing on the fringes of the institution, deriving no benefits of real community and fellowship from it, but still under its jurisdiction so it can load you with these petty restraints (you ought to be big enough to decide when you want to be non-involved), do for you? There was a time when this kind of crappy stuff was accepted under a mystique of obedience, but people aren't swallowing that shit any more. I see a tremendous trend today toward what I would call "the free church." Nuns who find they can't be true to their vocation within the institution, simply dissolving their ties with it and creating a free community life which won't be under these restrictions, and they can do the kind of community life and witness they believe in. By the same token, laymen pulling out of the parish to form free communities, house church groups, ecumenical parishes; simply moving ahead to do what is called for in our times but which the institutional leadership isn't willing to allow. Suggest you do likewise. The most Christian thing you could do for that chap is to tell him to go to hell.

It looks like we won't be coming by car to Cincinnati after all, so my hopes of a pleasant drive out your way won't be possible, at least for this round. I will have to fly to the Grail, then up to Oberlin for the Barth talk and then fly back to D.C. just in time to take 200 inner city children to Expo! Wow!! I think I will go somewhere and bury myself in the sand for a week when it is all over.

Love,
Rosemary

Dear Rosemary:

*L*ong time since your last letter. I am very interested in the new books, especially the Gregory one and, most of all, in your course on the theology of social change. Keep me posted on that one! I have been having trouble, just mechanical trouble, with the works and system in getting the books I need for my own work. Library red tape, etc. But I am coming along. The picture is slowly filling in. The Cargo syndrome, which people regard as confined to a few "savages," seems to be pretty universal. Throw out everything, all the "old" and all property, shell money, native clothes, etc., etc. Then wait for Cargo to come from land of dead (USA). Shake, quake, have visions, etc., while waiting. Cargo will come in form of complete magic technology that does everything for you and fills the huts with so many goodies you can no longer move. White man's Jesus religion was bum steer, because there was no Cargo. This one is the real stuff. In the end it tapers off into a kind of Melanesian secular city pitch, we have to work for it after all, let's try liberal politics. Meanwhile the guerillas are getting wised up. And so on.

Very good bit in your letter about my situation here. It is very unhealthy. I have thought about the various angles and still am. My present move is to try to get transferred to Chile. There the situation would be much better, at least. For the rest I still agree with you, but I'd need to talk about it more and see it clearer in this concrete case.

It is a pity you were not able to get down, but as it happened, that weekend I got a virus infection and was in no state to converse intelligently with anyone about anything. If you are going to be down this way again, I hope we can get together.

I can't write more now, but am most interested in your course which must be under way. Any notes or anything?

Love,
Tom

🍷

c. September 14, 1967

Dear Thomas:

*M*any thanks for your article. I must say that I find it very difficult to read those details. As a child of nine, the first pictures of the death camps were flashed across the American screens and news magazines, and it made an impression on me of terrible personal participation which has never departed. I suppose that is true of many — mostly the people personally scarred and emotionally involved were a bit older than I; although perhaps they (i.e., those 20–30 years old at the time of the "revelation") were more inclined to cover up their guilt, since they already had vested interest in the system that produced it.

I am fully prepared to believe that white people could do the same to Negroes here. However, I also am ashamed to admit that Black Militants might easily do the same to white people if they could ever get into power, which is unlikely. There was a time, even a few months ago, when I still had a kind of basic trust in the integrity and instinct for authenticity of Black radicals, but that is being disillusioned. Not that they are "worse than us," but they are the same as us, and are more and more attracted to doing over the same things we have done to them, only from their side. The dream of a "new creation" for our society is giving way to a kind of simple revenge and pyrrhic victory, in which black radicals enjoy the experience of calling the sons of the white middle class "boy." Everybody is playing games, and nobody is really taking humanity seriously. One of the big problems with the black community is that they have so little self-respect, which means to say each individual spends a lot of time pumping up his own image and identity, fluffing out his bush haircut, etc., but each black man has only contempt for the next black man. Because black men have no respect for each other, they dissipate their energies in infighting and winning psychological victories over "whitey" which leave them as psychologically (not to mention economically and politically) dependent on whitey as ever. Who is Rap Brown's lawyer? a black man? surely the man who wants nothing to do with the "honkey" would hire a black man for his lawyer, but no, not so, it is a white man, and so on.

My theology of social change will go back into 19th century Christian socialism, the American social gospel, move on up through the Niebuhr social realism school, the church renewal people (Gibson Winter), secular city types, Christian Marxists, new left, Black power, Hippies. That is the itinerary, but what we will see on the journey is another matter. I really don't know. There is such a plethora of good will and good ideology floating around and such a dearth of ability to create and guide meaningful social change. Nobody really knows how ideologies are translated into meaningful exercise — often it is more accidental than anything else when some advance is actually made even though a particular group may claim a victory for their "ideology." The Marxist experience hasn't done much either to enlighten us or reassure us on this score. It does seem that our society is coming to a boil, and something is going to happen, but the ideologies are as much by-products as guides to the actual nature and direction of the overflow. Like you I am not inclined to disregard the possibility that the people who may eventually fall heir to all this "left" turmoil will not be "left" people at all, but the right wing, the ever present fascist stratum in American society, who may well be the ones who will harness and drive the revolution. Witness how easily SDS rhetoric of government by the people can be translated into a speech by Ronald Reagan. The right wing knows how to organize and use power — and they have money — the new left have none of these things — all they have are big mouths, and big hearts, neither of which is accomplishing very much.

What is in Chile? I am glad you are thinking of some new step. I have had such a strong feeling that your situation was at a breaking point, and some change, almost any change, was called for rather than standing pat. But then you put up such a fight and protested so vigorously that I didn't know what to think — as though you were afraid someone was going to use you — you probably see too many sides of the issue at once — that is the trouble with people with broad perspectives — they can't make decisions — it helps to be simple minded sometimes.

Love,
Rosemary

※※

Late December 1967

Dear Brother:

*Y*ou are really a shocking and dissolute fellow. Didn't anyone ever tell you that the one thing a good son of the church never, never does, especially in ecclesiastical assemblies, is to state the bald unregenerate truth? Surely someone must have pointed this elementary fact out to you sometime during your novitiate. I have a very good poem written by a friend of mine that, allowing for a change of gender, will well describe your particular state of moral turpitude, and if I can find it, I will send you a copy. It talks about what my friend will do when she is old and says some very good things about what happens to such obnoxious persons — the last lines as I remember them go like this:

I suppose with such views I shall be
left quite alone
To mumble plain truths like a dog
mumbling a bone

As for your drawings, I do not have much good to report. Early in the year very elaborate plans were worked out by Mr. Pauker for an exhibit, which would include your drawings and some welded sculptures made by prison inmates. Mr. Pauker had very elaborate plans for an elegant show, all kinds of Washington notables were to be there, much expensive food would be distributed, and hopefully much money flow in — he also had elaborate plans as to how this money would be split up, a generous hunk to himself for tax purposes, which he then insisted he would pass back again to the prison inmates. We were very dubious and didn't know quite what to make of this little man in the pink suit, but we tried to go along and tailor the plan to the realities of our situation and our purposes and make safeguards against misuse. Plans were made for a Christmas exhibit in Georgetown managed by our board for the community centre which handles our neighborhood programs. However, at the crucial moment it turned out that Mr. Pauker's plan was pure chimera; he did not, in fact, have any such prison sculptures at his disposal, although he had given us to understand that he had commissioned such. His list of notables may also have been equally illusionary — at least the people he claimed to have contacted did not seem to have heard of him. So the exhibit was folded up by us very rapidly. We still had some vague ideas of putting on a show of your things, but this is not formulated at all at present. If I were you, I would simply extract your drawings from Mr. Pauker before they all disappear. I don't want to accuse him, but he really is a puzzle, and we don't know what to make of him at all. If you want a good group that would exhibit them and have them really seen by a good set of people in Washington who are interested in meaningful things, I would suggest the little religious art bookstore called "The Sign of Jonah." It is run by the Community of Christ, which is an ecumenical covenanted community in the Dupont Circle area. If you give the go ahead, I will try to get the drawings transferred over there. They are presently exhibiting Corita's drawings.[31]

All best for the coming year.

Love,
Rosemary

December 31, 1967

Dear Rosemary:

Ah, yes, I have become very wicked. This is due in great part to my hanging around with these women theologians. What a downfall. Let others be warned in time. Young priests can never be too careful. Tsk. Tsk.

About the drawings: what you say about our friend fully confirms the impressions that have been growing on me from one direction or other. I don't want to get in a sordid little struggle over it. But I do want the drawings to be in the hands of someone who is not looking at them through that particular color spectacles.

Why don't I do it this way: I make a gift of all the drawings of mine that are in the "Fun House" (inauspicious name from the start) to your parish. They now (if the parish accepts) belong to the parish, and you all can do what you want with them: sell them any way convenient or hang them up or give them away, and what you absolutely don't want or can't be bothered with just send on to Bellarmine College collect. (To the Dean, Fr. John Loftus). As

31. Sister Corita Kent, I.H.M., a popular artist who colorfully illustrated posters, books, and even gas holding tanks near Boston.

to the wording of the above, frame it any way you want so that you can get the pictures loose from the man (who is probably selling them on the side and pocketing all the money anyhow). The drawings are yours. Unfortunately, I don't have an inventory of them, but there must be about twenty available still. But get whatever you can. As to the rest, I really don't care. Notables! Yah! It was ever so.

Last time I wrote I forgot to tell you about two books which are essential for your course, if you haven't found them already: Peter Worsley, *The Trumpet Shall Sound* and Burridge, *Mambu,* both on the Cargo cults. Both excellent. I have a tape I made on Cargo cults floating around somewhere (I sent it first to our monastery in Georgia, now it may be around Washington, not sure). If you are interested, I can get it to you before it makes the circle and comes back. Haven't got anything on paper about Cargo yet, except parts of a long poem I am writing about things like Cargo, the Ghost Dance, Indian revolts in Yucatan, etc. I'll send a piece on the latter while I am at it now.

Big rush to answer some mail, so will quit now, with love in the Lord,

Tom

A Round and a Hope for Smithgirls

Children the time of angry Fathers
Is torn off the calendar
They turn to shadows in the spring

The city that they thought was theirs they surrender
To the gentle Children that were
Made unhappy in the electric flood
And emptiness

So believe him alone
The gentle One
That you yourselves are

Believe yourselves
Unspoken arguments of a very poor
God who has got lost in the
City of squares
Out of a job again and looking for his arm

Lost and looking for a believable joy
To surface in the tame eyes
Of all who are his own

Of all who may be mirrors
Of his lost way
In angry walks to the elevator
Mad at the failed lights

O they leave you alone
And it is all right

Look
All the windows are now awake
And yours O Flowers!

Thomas Merton

c. January 31, 1968

Dear Thomas:

I picked up the drawings the other day from Pauker. I think he sold 5 or 6 — I have 29. But he also put money into fine frames on some of them, so I don't know what to do about an accounting on the ones sold. He said nothing about it. Perhaps I should just leave it.

I am getting into my course on theology of social change. There is so much, and I am very much a novice in many of these areas. I expect to read a great deal this semester and try to work out quite finished talks for each Monday night lecture (2½ hours). I will also use some of the same material for two events this summer: a 4 week lecture series at a Lutheran place in Northern Washington (Holden Village) and a four day symposium at Holy Cross Abbey in Canon, Colorado where I will share with Bernard Häring, Roland Murphy and Martin Marty.

I just got an offer to be nominated for President of the Catholic Theological Society — and turned it down. I must say I am a little bemused by the eagerness of various Catholic quarters for my name and presence. I wonder whether they have really read what I am writing or whether I am just a balloon on the horizon that they are clutching at.

Best,
Rosemary

February 18, 1968

Dear Rosemary:

*T*hanks for picking up the drawings. As a matter of fact I paid Pauker everything he paid out for frames and I suspect a little more (I have a feeling he charged me for a rebate that the framer gave him). Doesn't matter. But if he sold any pictures you are entitled to the proceeds. I leave you to judge whether you want to go into the unpleasantness, and in any case, he will probably — such is my guess — find some way of giving you about half of what you ought to get. The important thing is that the drawings are out of his hands.

The things scheduled for you for next summer sound worth while. I agree with you about the theologians and think you were smart not to accept. You are now an image, and if you don't look out they'll use you to comfort them in all kinds of irrationalities. Every once in a while we have to do a little iconoclasm in our own back yard.

Well, not even the new Abbot is going to send me to Chile, but he will at least let me go to things that are normal for a monk to go to. I may have a chance to get some fairly interesting meetings abroad. Or if the meetings are not interesting, maybe I can see some worthwhile people on the side. But I don't anticipate getting around much and don't really care — at least not for the nonsense and ritual of conferences.

Take care of yourself.
All my best, always,
Tom

AFTERWORD

by Christine Bochen

O ne wonders what Thomas Merton might have said about his correspondence with Rosemary Radford Ruether had he been able to reflect on their exchange a quarter of a century later. Though that is something we will never know, it is clear that at the time Merton corresponded with Ruether he found her an engaging, exacting, and sometimes unrelenting dialogue partner. They soon fell into a spirited, even heated, debate that ranged over a variety of topics but returned again and again to subjects that had great personal significance for Merton: monasticism, the role of the monk in the contemporary world, the relationship of the church and the world, contemplation and solitude. Their correspondence reveals much about Merton, both about what he thought and who he was.

In August 1966, when Merton first heard from Rosemary Radford Ruether, she was a young and promising Catholic theologian teaching at George Washington and Howard Universities and looking forward to the publication of her first book, *The Church against Itself.* Thomas Merton was a Trappist monk at the Abbey of Gethsemani, where he had lived for almost twenty-five years, and a well-known and well-published writer. His autobiography, *The Seven Storey Mountain,* which appeared in 1940, quickly became a best-seller and thrust the young monk into the public eye — a most unexpected turn of events for a Trappist. With subsequent books and countless essays and reviews, Merton established himself as a spiritual writer who introduced readers to the rich heritage of monastic wisdom and invited them to experience for themselves a contemplative spirituality. He became for many nothing less than a "spiritual master." In the sixties, he challenged readers, pleasing some, disappointing and angering others, with controversial writings on war and peace, racism and justice, technology and humanism. Driven by his passion for truth, Merton felt compelled to voice his opposition to the proliferation of nuclear weapons, the injustice of racism, and the immorality of the war in Vietnam. He was equally outspoken in his criticism of those in the Roman Catholic Church who kept their silence in the face of social evils that threatened to destroy humankind. He disapproved of a monastic culture that stubbornly clung to old ways and refused to cast off rigid and lifeless practice. As monk and writer, Merton assumed a critical, one might say, prophetic role challenging social, ecclesial, and monastic institutions alike.

Though Merton was clear in his fidelity to truth and freedom, he struggled, as we all do, to discern what truth and freedom required of him in his own life. "Being a Catholic and being a monk have not always been easy," he wrote on January 22, 1967. Merton certainly had his share of crises, perhaps more than his share. He agonized over how he could reconcile being a monk and a writer; he endured periods of spiritual dryness; he experienced conflicts with superiors, whose vision of the monastic vocation differed from his own, and he strained under the burden of censorship. All the while he hungered for deeper silence and solitude than life at Gethsemani afforded him. He even considered going elsewhere to live as a monk — perhaps to a Carthusian or Camaldolese foundation, or even to Latin America. Even when, in 1965, he finally was granted permission to live in a hermitage on the grounds of the monastery, he continued to be troubled by how accessible he was and how vulnerable to intrusions (though it was part of the paradox of his character that, not infrequently, he seemed to welcome these intrusions). In 1968, the year he died, with the permission of a new abbot he was able to travel to New Mexico, Alaska, and California; during his trips he kept his eyes open for sites that might be appropriate locations for a hermitage. In 1966, he fell in love with a nursing student assigned to care for him while he was hospitalized in Louisville. He struggled to affirm the true beauty and deep meaning of their love while confirming once again his commitment to the monastic life.

Though his readers may have looked upon Merton's life as idyllic, it was hardly so. His crises, recounted in *The Sign of Jonas* and well documented in his letters, were very deep and very real. In an essay, published in *Contemplation in a World of Action*, Merton describes himself as "a self-questioning human person, who like his brothers [and sisters] struggles to cope with turbulent, mysterious, demanding, exciting, frustrating existence." It is a candid and very apt description. In many ways, throughout his life, Merton felt like an outsider, an alien in his monastery, his church, and his society. Yet beneath the turmoil and anguish, there was a deep source from which Merton drew courage and strength. That source was contemplation, a deep awareness and experience of God. It was his spirituality that sustained him; it was in solitude and in silence that he found himself to be most at home. He was convinced that the monastic life was the life for him and he reaffirmed, time and again, that being a monk was who he was.

But what did it mean to be a monk? That was a question to which Merton returned again and again. Over the years his thinking developed in ways that amounted to dramatic conversions. The monk who had sought refuge from the world when he entered the monastery in 1941 discovered in the 1950s and 1960s that there was no leaving the world. His definition of what it meant to be a monk grew from seeing himself as a monk against the world to recognizing that he was a monk in and for the world.

While Ruether and Merton were corresponding, Merton was

struggling with issues of monastic renewal, not just intellectually but personally. Indeed Merton, whose theology was deeply rooted in experience, especially in his experience of God, engaged in issues in a way that was personal. Talk about monasticism and the role of the monk in the modern world was not a theoretical discussion for Merton. No wonder then that he was, as these letters show, defensive in the face of Ruether's penetrating and clearly negative appraisal of the value of monasticism as it was being lived in the modern world. And though Merton himself was critical of the rigidity of monasticism and convinced that it was in need of reform, he was thoroughly committed to the viability of the monastic life in the contemporary world. It was precisely this view that Ruether challenged and the exchange that ensued makes this correspondence so engaging.

In many ways, Thomas Merton's correspondence with Rosemary Radford Ruether was typical of exchanges Merton had with so many others. And there were many others: Merton's published letters comprise five hefty volumes. His list of correspondents included people all over the world: Europe and the Soviet Union, the Middle East, the Far East, Latin America. Among them were philosophers and writers, popes and presidents, monks and activists, theologians and psychologists — quite an amazing and extensive circle for a monk. Merton's correspondence with Ruether began with a request for him to read a manuscript, which met with his enthusiastic reply and led to his request that she "send along anything that would be good for me." Ideas about topics of mutual interest were passed back and forth as were suggestions for reading. There were areas of agreement and areas of sharp disagreement, which made for lively debate. Ruether challenged Merton in a way few others did. While she was not the first or only correspondent to question the meaning of monasticism or to challenge the value of his lifestyle, she was certainly a most formidable adversary. Especially in the 1960s when Merton's circle of correspondents came to include writers and poets who knew little of monastic life, Merton developed a way to explain his choice to be a monk. He did so in a-religious terms, presenting himself as a hippie-hermit of sorts, labeling himself a non-monk, living an "ordinary life" in the woods. He explains himself to Ruether, who questions a life of withdrawal when the world is so greatly in need of socially engaged Christians, in this way: "I am a notorious maverick in the Order. . . . My hermit life is expressly a *lay* life." Ruether is not so easily satisfied and presses Merton to consider leaving the monastery and to "come on in" and become part of the struggle, part of the action of the church.

Though Merton was open to Ruether, willing to learn from her, receptive to the challenges inherent in her critique of monasticism, respectful of her engagement and commitment, he was adamant in his conviction that the monastic life — for all its struggles and ambiguities — was nevertheless the place for him.

These letters, which reveal some of what was in Merton's mind during a very significant time in his life, testify to his firm commitment to the most fundamental of all Cistercian vows: stability. It was his way of being at home in the world.

INDEX